INTERNATIONAL POPULISM

DUNCAN McDONNELL
ANNIKA WERNER

# International Populism

*The Radical Right in the European Parliament*

**OXFORD**
UNIVERSITY PRESS

# OXFORD
UNIVERSITY PRESS

Oxford University Press is a department of the
University of Oxford. It furthers the University's objective
of excellence in research, scholarship, and education
by publishing worldwide.

Oxford   New York
Auckland   Cape Town   Dar es Salaam   Hong Kong   Karachi
Kuala Lumpur   Madrid   Melbourne   Mexico City   Nairobi
New Delhi   Shanghai   Taipei   Toronto

With offices in
Argentina   Austria   Brazil   Chile   Czech Republic   France   Greece
Guatemala   Hungary   Italy   Japan   Poland   Portugal   Singapore
South Korea   Switzerland   Thailand   Turkey   Ukraine   Vietnam

Oxford is a registered trade mark of Oxford University Press
in the UK and certain other countries.

Published in the United States of America by
Oxford University Press
198 Madison Avenue, New York, NY 10016

Copyright © Duncan Mcdonnell and Annika Werner 2019

All rights reserved. No part of this publication may be reproduced,
stored in a retrieval system, or transmitted, in any form or by any means,
without the prior permission in writing of Oxford University Press,
or as expressly permitted by law, by license, or under terms agreed with
the appropriate reproduction rights organization. Inquiries concerning
reproduction outside the scope of the above should be sent to the
Rights Department, Oxford University Press, at the address above.

You must not circulate this work in any other form
and you must impose this same condition on any acquirer.

Library of Congress Cataloging-in-Publication Data is available
Duncan Mcdonnell and Annika Werner.
International Populism: The Radical Right in the European Parliament.
ISBN: 9780197500859

Printed in the United Kingdom on acid-free paper
by Bell and Bain Ltd, Glasgow

*Annika dedicates this book to her mother, Hella.*
*Duncan dedicates this book to his parents, Pat and Phyllis.*

# CONTENTS

*Acknowledgements* ix
*List of Tables and Figures* xi

1. International Populism — 1
2. Radical Right Populists and Group Formation in the European Parliament — 19
3. European Conservatives and Reformists — 55
4. Europe of Freedom and Direct Democracy — 93
5. Europe of Nations and Freedom — 127
6. Radical Right Populists Inside and Outside the European Parliament — 161
7. From International Populism to Transnational Populism — 197

Appendix: List of Interviewees — 231

*Notes* 235
*Bibliography* 249
*Index* 261

# ACKNOWLEDGEMENTS

Without the counsel and helpful comments of many colleagues, this book would not have come to fruition. We would like to thank Niklas Bolin, Lucas Dolan, Diego Fossati, Reinhard Heinisch, Zoe Lefkofridi, Benjamin Leruth, Marta Lorimer, Gary Marks, Ferran Martinez i Coma, Lee Morgenbesser, Matt Wood and the two anonymous reviewers who have all helped improve and enrich the content of this book.

Furthermore, we have benefitted greatly from the opportunity to present findings at the UC Berkeley Center for Right-Wing Studies, the City University of New York Comparative Politics workshop, the Center for European Studies at the University of North Carolina (Chapel Hill), the MacMillan Center at Yale University, the Department of Political Science at the University of Copenhagen, the Department of Politics at the University of Turin, the OECD in Paris, C-Rex at the University of Oslo, the Centre for European Research at Queen Mary University of London, the Crick Centre at the University of Sheffield, the Sydney

## ACKNOWLEDGEMENTS

Democracy Network at the University of Sydney and the Department of Political Science and Sociology at the University of Salzburg. The participants at numerous conference panels over the past four years have also provided invaluable comments. At Griffith University, we would like to thank Dr Malin Karlsson, a postdoctoral fellow, as well as Diego Leiva, Melodie Ruwet and Pandanus Petter, all doctoral students, for their assistance with the research. We would also like to express our deep gratitude to the many party representatives and officials from across Europe who were extremely generous with their time and insights. Finally, we would like to thank the European Commission's Marie Curie Fellowship program, the Centre for Governance and Public Policy at Griffith University, and the Australian Research Council's Discovery Projects scheme for their support of different elements and stages of this project.

# LIST OF TABLES AND FIGURES

## Tables

| | |
|---|---|
| Table 1.1: Radical Right Populists in the 2014–2019 European Parliament | 7 |
| Table 2.1: The main radical right populist parties of ECR, EFDD and ENF since 1999 | 30 |
| Table 3.1: Main members of ECR | 58 |
| Table 3.2: Positions on immigration and deviation within ECR | 65 |
| Table 3.3: Financial resources per MEP, EFDD and ECR 2017 | 70 |
| Table 4.1: Main members of EFDD | 96 |
| Table 4.2: Positions on immigration and deviation within EFDD | 102 |
| Table 4.3: Financial resources per MEP, ENF and EFDD 2017 | 106 |
| Table 5.1: Main members of ENF | 129 |
| Table 5.2: Positions on immigration and deviation within ENF | 139 |

| | | |
|---|---|---|
| Table 5.3: | Financial resources per MEP, ENF and EFDD 2017 | 143 |
| Table 6.1: | Group cohesion by policy area | 169 |
| Table 6.2: | Loyalty of individual parties to groups | 171 |
| Table 6.3: | Rapporteurs 2014–2019 | 174 |
| Table 6.4: | Press release analysis, six months before national election | 181 |
| Table 6.5: | Party switches between groups, July 2014-January 2019 | 188 |
| Table 7.1: | The two most important issues facing our country | 224 |
| Table 7.2: | The two most important issues facing the EU | 226 |

## Figures

| | | |
|---|---|---|
| Figure 3.1: | ECR parties 2009 and 2014, European integration | 63 |
| Figure 3.2: | ECR parties 2009 and 2014, left-right positions | 66 |
| Figure 4.1: | EFDD and ENF parties 2014, European integration | 100 |
| Figure 4.2: | EFDD and ENF parties 2014, left-right positions | 103 |
| Figure 5.1: | ENF parties 2009 and 2014, European integration | 137 |
| Figure 5.2: | ENF parties 2009 and 2014, left-right positions | 140 |

# LIST OF TABLES AND FIGURES

Figure 6.1: Group cohesion in the EP 2014–2018     167

Figure 7.1: Positions of nine radical right populist parties in 2014     202

# 1

# INTERNATIONAL POPULISM

Radical right populism is on the rise internationally. From the United States to India, from Brazil to Italy, radical right populist leaders and parties are doing better than ever electorally and, increasingly, are entering government. If in some areas of the globe their rise has been sudden, their recent achievements in Western Europe follow decades of successes and setbacks, but, ultimately, continued presence and growth. Countries like France, Italy, Belgium and Austria have had radical right populist (RRP) parties since the 1970s and 1980s. Not only have they survived, but a new generation of leaders such as Marine Le Pen of the Front National (FN—National Front), Matteo Salvini of the Lega Nord (LN—Northern League), and Kristian Thulesen Dahl of the Dansk Folkeparti (DF—Danish People's Party) has shown that these parties can outlast charismatic founder-leaders and thrive.[1] Meanwhile, countries we previously thought immune to radical right populism, such as

Sweden, Germany and Spain, have proven us wrong over the last decade.[2]

Radical right populists in most of Western Europe are exerting greater influence than ever and it seems they are here to stay. Having once been seen as sporadic and marginal pariahs, they are now counted amongst the largest, and sometimes the ruling, parties in their countries. This has raised questions about their effects on politics nationally and internationally.

One issue that has received particular interest over the past five years is the extent to which radical right populists co-operate with one another in the European Union's elected representative body, the European Parliament (EP). This book seeks to understand and explain that co-operation. Which alliances do radical right populists form in the EP? What are the logics underpinning them? How and why have they changed over time? What does international co-operation mean for these parties and how does it function inside and outside parliament? And finally, what does all of this tell us about the past, present and future of one of the key phenomena affecting politics in twenty-first century Europe?

The upsurge in attention paid to international populist co-operation can be traced back to 13 November 2013, when the FN leader Marine Le Pen and Geert Wilders of the Dutch Partij voor de Vrijheid (PVV— Party for Freedom) announced in The Hague that their parties would form the core of a prospective new EP group after the European elections in May 2014.[3] In the months that followed, scholars and commentators speculated about how radical right populist parties would perform electorally, how many of them would band together in parliament and what impact they might have.[4] This represented a new and exciting element (finally!) in European Parliament politics. Radical right populists had long been the 'odd ones out' in the EP when compared to the other party families of Christian Democrats, Social Democrats, Liberals, the Radical Left and Greens. The latter all fit the main theoretical explanation for EP alliances of 'policy congruence' and tend to sit together in lasting and relatively stable groups (McElroy and Benoit 2010, 2011). Or, to put it another way, European ideological birds of a feather tend to flock (and stay) together. Radical right populists traditionally have not done this. Instead, they have usually either been dispersed into small, short-lived, ideologically heterogeneous groups that are 'marriages of convenience' (to secure funding) or they have been isolated among the parliament's non-inscrits (non-aligned). Of the few EP groups before 2014 that had had radical right populists among their leading members, none had remained intact beyond a single legislature (and others had been much shorter lived).

Reflecting this history of disunity, the prevailing view among academics for many years was that radical right populists in the EP were 'unlikely bedfellows' due to mutual antipathy, fear of being tainted by association and conflicting nationalist agendas (Fieschi 2000; Startin 2010). Thus, Minkenberg and Perrineau (2007: 51) concluded just over a decade ago that, in the EP, 'there is nothing more difficult to establish than an international group of nationalists'.

So, does that still hold true? Are radical right populists still the odd ones out in the European Parliament? In this book, we explore what actually happened after the 2014 election, when seventy-three of the 751 elected Members of the European Parliament (MEPs) were radical right populists, their highest number to date.[5] We explain the parliamentary alliances they formed and what they mean for our understanding of these parties today. Our focus is therefore on the three groups in the 2014–2019 parliament that contained radical right populists: European Conservatives and Reformists (ECR), Europe of Freedom and Direct Democracy (EFDD) and Europe of Nations and Freedom (ENF).

The UK Conservative-led ECR included in 2014 the Danish People's Party and the Finnish Perussuomalaiset (PS—Finns Party), alongside less radical and non-populist right-wing parties. The EFDD, dominated by the UK Independence Party (UKIP), brought in the Swedish Sverigedemokraterna (SD—Sweden Democrats), along with a mixture of non-radical right MEPs, including those from the Italian Movimento Cinque Stelle (M5S—Five Star Movement). Finally, the ENF created in June 2015 the largest ideologically homogenous radical right populist group in the parliament there had ever been up until that point. This brought together the Front National, the Dutch Party for Freedom, the Northern League, the Austrian Freiheitliche Partei Österreichs (FPÖ—Austrian Freedom Party) and the Flemish Vlaams Belang (VB—Flemish Interest). These nine ECR, EFDD and ENF parties, which are listed below in Table 1.1, have all been consistently recognised as radical right populist parties in the literature by contemporary scholars (e.g. Mudde 2019; Rooduijn et al. 2019) and are the only radical right populist parties in 2014/15 to have joined EP groups.

Looking at Table 1.1 (p. 7), the reader might wonder why we do not include other parties which gained MEPs in 2014, such as the Polish Prawo i Sprawiedliwość (PiS—Law and Justice), the Alternative für Deutschland (AfD—Alternative for Germany), the Greek Chrysí Avgí (Golden Dawn), the Hungarian Jobbik Magyarországért Mozgalom (Movement for a Better Hungary, commonly known simply as 'Jobbik'), or Hungary's ruling party Fidesz. There are a number of reasons for this. First, we share the widely-held view that Golden Dawn is a neo-fascist, rather than a radical right populist, party and therefore we do not consider it (Ellinas 2015; Vasilopoulou and Halikiopoulou 2015). Second, while Jobbik has been considered 'radical right' (i.e. democratic) rather than 'extreme right' (anti-democratic) by experts for many years (e.g. Pirro 2015; Pytlas 2016), all of the radical right parties in our study have shunned it. As a result, Jobbik, like Golden Dawn, spent the legislature amongst the non-inscrits. Since we want to understand why radical right populists join particular groups, they are therefore of less interest (although we do discuss briefly in Chapter 5 the reasons for Jobbik's exclusion by its former allies in the FN).[6] We also omit from our main analysis two ECR parties that were not commonly recognised by scholars as radical right populist in the period around the 2014 elections, namely the Polish PiS and the German AfD, even though both had a radical right populist 'turn' in subsequent years (Arzheimer 2015; Stanley and Cześnik 2019). However, since both were in the ECR, we did conduct interviews with MEPs from the two parties and include this material (where relevant) in this book. Finally, we faced the question of how to treat Fidesz. Given that Fidesz's longstanding (albeit controversial) membership of the European People's Party continued during the 2014–2019 parliament and the disagreement among scholars surrounding its classification as 'radical right populist' during this period, we do not discuss its group strategies in this book.[7] However, since we believe that Fidesz—like PiS and the AfD—had become a fully radical right populist party by the end of the legislature, we do consider the roles of these parties within the broader radical right populist family in the post-2019 parliament in the course of drawing our conclusions.

Table 1.1: Radical Right Populists in the 2014–2019 European Parliament

| Party | Country | EP Group | 2014 Vote % | MEPs |
|---|---|---|---|---|
| Danish People's Party | Denmark | ECR | 26.6 | 4 |
| Finns Party | Finland | ECR | 12.9 | 2 |
| UKIP | UK | EFDD | 27.5 | 24 |
| Sweden Democrats | Sweden | EFDD* | 9.7 | 2 |
| National Front | France | ENF | 24.9 | 23** |
| Northern League | Italy | ENF | 6.2 | 5 |
| Party for Freedom | Netherlands | ENF | 13.3 | 4 |
| Austrian Freedom Party | Austria | ENF | 19.7 | 4 |
| Flemish Interest | Belgium | ENF | 4.3 | 1 |

Note: Votes in percentages. Number of MEPs at first session of the new EP in July 2014.

\* The Sweden Democrats moved from the EFDD to ECR in July 2018.

\*\* The FN lost one MEP to the EFDD before parliament sat for the first time.

Our explanations of radical right populist alliances and actions in the EP are based on a mixture of qualitative and quantitative methods (see Chapter 2). As regards the former, we believe this is the first study to have enjoyed access to senior figures in so many different European radical right populist parties (see the appendix for the full list of interviewees). From June 2014, immediately after the elections and when EP groups were being created, until November 2018, when the legislature was nearing its end, we conducted interviews with thirty-one key national and European-level figures from all of the nine RRP parties shown in Table 1.1 and their main non-radical right partners (such as the UK Conservatives and the M5S). In a number of cases, we interviewed the same people at different points during the parliamentary term to get their perspectives over time.

We complement this extensive interview material with party position data from the 2009 and 2014 waves of the Chapel Hill Expert Survey (Bakker et al., 2015). Specifically, we compare the parties' positions on two key RRP policy areas, immigration and Euroscepticism, in addition to the social and economic left–right dimensions, which structure the space of European party competition generally (Marks et al. 2006). We also consider the salience that parties attributed to these issues. Finally, we use EP voting data and press releases to examine the policy fit between parties, how they have acted in the EP and how they have presented (and used) their international alliances domestically.

'This is all well and good', you might say, 'but who really cares about what parties do in the European Parliament? Most citizens in the EU do not bother to vote in European elections and even those that do have little knowledge of what happens in Brussels and

Strasbourg'. This is all true. Until 2019 when it rose back to just above 50 per cent, turnout declined at every single EP election after 1979, hitting a new low of 42.6 per cent in 2014.[8] And, as our interviews with radical right populist and mainstream politicians conducted for this book reveal, most of them acknowledge that their grassroots members and the wider public have little idea about their allies in the EP. Indeed, one current radical right populist party leader even told us that, when he was first elected to national parliament in 2011, he did not know with whom his party sat in the EP![9]

This perceived lack of importance may explain the lack of attention that European-level politics has received within the vast literature on radical right populism. As Cas Mudde (2016: 2) notes, since the early 1980s, more articles and books have been written about right-wing populist parties than all other ideological party types combined. And yet, while researchers such as Almeida (2010), Brack (2015), Bolin (2015), Bressanelli (2012), Fieschi (2000), Leruth (2017), Startin (2010) and Whitaker and Lynch (2014) have produced extremely useful articles and book chapters that discuss radical right populist parties and their elected representatives in the EP, ours is the first book-length study on the topic.

Of course, just because something has not been done before does not mean that it should be done. There are often good reasons why, to use a hackneyed academic phrase, 'a gap in the literature' exists and why it should probably persist. However, as we show in the chapters that follow, an examination of EP group choices and actions can tell us a great deal about how parties see themselves, how they want to be seen by others, how other parties actually do see them, and where parties are going both nationally and internationally. In a period when radical right populists are transitioning from being marginal to becoming major parties throughout Europe, this perspective may be especially useful.

Take, for example, the Sweden Democrats, a party with an extreme right-wing history, which entered national parliament in 2010 and the EP in 2014. In the 2018 Swedish general election, the party finished third, just a couple of percentage points behind the main Swedish centre-right party.[10] As we explain in Chapter 4, despite previous good relations with the Front National, the Sweden Democrats decided not to join the ENF group due to the perceived domestic image costs of being associated with FN and the Austrian Freedom Party. They were then themselves rebuffed—for precisely the same reasons—in their attempt to join the Danish People's Party and Finns Party in the more moderate ECR. Interviewees from the UK Conservatives told us how they drew a clear distinction between the SD and the other two Nordic radical right populist parties based on their very different histories—something the Danish People's Party and Finns Party, eager to polish their own domestic images and please their new mainstream European partners, heartily agreed with. Eventually, the SD were accepted into the UKIP-led EFDD on the grounds that UKIP needed the numbers to form a group and were reassured that the Sweden Democrats would not damage their reputation in Britain.

The Sweden Democrats in mid-2014 thus preferred an ideologically heterogenous group (the EFDD, which contained the Five Star Movement) over their 'natural home' in the more homogenous ENF, whose parties shared their positions on immigration and other key issues. As a leading SD representative explained to us, they decided to forsake policy congruence with what he termed 'all those good parties' in the ENF, because they were playing a two-level game in which European-level behaviour was considered to have potential domestic advantages and disadvantages—and they had a general election coming up in September 2014. Four years later, the same mechanism was applied. No longer content with the mere 'marriage of convenience' offered by the EFDD, in July 2018, several months before that year's Swedish general election, the Sweden Democrats secured a 'respectable marriage' with the ECR, as the veto power of the Brexit-bound Conservatives waned and the Danish People's Party and Finns Party shifted their positions on SD entry to strong support (inspired, they told us, by the party's good behaviour since 2014, but also by its electoral growth). This series of actions and reactions helps us understand the trajectory and mainstreaming goals of the Sweden Democrats, how they leverage the European level to achieve those goals, and the logics shaping other radical right populists' and mainstream parties' approaches to international partnerships.

We believe that, through these and other accounts of why radical right populists behave as they do at European level, our study makes an important theoretical and empirical contribution to our understanding of RRP parties today. While other ideological party types have followed the logic of 'birds of a feather flock together', and allied in broadly policy-congruent EP groups (McElroy and Benoit 2010, 2011; Bressanelli 2012), radical right populists have often been isolated and/or shunned one another. This is changing. Based on our findings, we argue that radical right populists in the EP came of age, albeit in various ways, after 2014, whether as 'respectable radicals' able to secure mainstream alliances (e.g. the Sweden Democrats) or as 'proud populists' now embracing their commonalities and sharing a mission to 'save Europe' (e.g. the Dutch PVV). There may not (yet) be a 'Populist International', but radical right populists are reasoning and co-operating internationally, just like 'normal' parties do. And, increasingly, more than 'normal' parties do. As we explain in the conclusions, while radical right populists in Europe until recently have focused on national concerns and campaigns, we believe that the international, and transnational, character of their appeals and alliances will become a more important feature of these parties in the years to come.

*Structure*

The book proceeds as follows: in Chapter 2, 'Radical right populists and group formation in the European Parliament', we firstly discuss our core concept of 'radical right populism'. We then give an overview of the history of RRP co-operation (and mostly non-co-operation) in the EP, before setting out our theoretical framework explaining EP group formation. This is an adaptation of the national coalition explanation along the lines of 'policy', 'office', and 'votes' (Müller and Strøm 1990). Since there is broad agreement in the literature that the main driver of alliances at European level is policy congruence (McElroy and Benoit 2010, 2011; Bressanelli 2012), we devote considerable attention throughout the book to assessing the extent to which radical right populists follow this logic. Finally, we explain the data used to test this theoretical framework and expand it to accommodate the EP-specific mechanisms.

The next three chapters focus on the three EP groups that include radical right populists: the ECR, the EFDD and the ENF. In all three chapters, we first use Chapel Hill Expert Survey data on party positions to assess the fit of parties in 2014 regarding key policies (immigration, European integration, social and economic left–right issues). We then examine the role that office considerations might have played in determining group choices. The third step of our analysis focuses on the motivations of individual parties to join their respective groups rather than others. Questions arising, for example, in Chapter 3 include why the ECR parties were willing to let the Danish People's Party and Finns Party join them in 2014, having declined their applications in 2009.

Chapter 4 turns to the EFDD and considers why UKIP ruled out an EP alliance with the French Front National and the ENF parties in 2014, but was willing to accept the Sweden Democrats who have a similar—and more recent—'extreme right' history to FN. Regarding the ENF, in Chapter 5 we investigate why this group of high-profile radical right populist parties came together when they did, and how they resolved the long-standing RRP conundrum of reconciling their defence of national interests with international co-operation.

On the basis of these analyses, we propose multiple theoretical insights. In Chapter 3, we advance our 'respectable radicals' theory of EP group formation. In other words, we argue that the Danish People's Party and Finns Party (like the Sweden Democrats) played a two-level game in 2014 whereby they valued the perceived domestic 'office' and 'votes' benefits of EP alliances more highly than 'policy congruence' at the

European level. This explains not only why they did not want to be associated with parties like the Front National and the Austrian Freedom Party, but also why the DF and PS left UKIP's group in 2014 to move to the more moderate, Conservative-led ECR. For the Danes and Finns, their admission into the ECR marked a 'coming of age' milestone in terms of their legitimation and development. The rationale behind the EFDD, on the other hand, was first and foremost that of 'a marriage of convenience' in order to secure the EP group spoils (i.e. financial/administrative resources and the visibility offered by extra speaking time).

Our findings about the ENF provide an insight into the future of radical right populist co-operation, at least for some parties, both inside and outside the EP. Our interviews show the creation of the ENF also represented a 'coming of age' for these RRPs, albeit very different from that of the 'respectable radicals' discussed previously. The ENF 'coming of age' reflected the desire to create a lasting European group composed of radical right populist parties unashamed of their commonalities. Instead of seeking legitimacy by allying with more mainstream parties, the ENF parties embraced their shared values. Moreover, they squared the circle of being an 'international group of nationalists' by presenting themselves not only as defenders of their own nations, but of a wider 'European' people against the supposedly increasing threats posed by EU elites and dangerous 'others', especially Islam. In this way, we argue that these parties bridge international populism and transnational populism (Moffitt 2017: 410; de Cleen 2017).

Having explained RRP group formation choices and strategies, Chapter 6, 'Radical Right Populists Inside and Outside the European Parliament', identifies events in the ensuing years that can shed light on the stability of these groups and their utility for RRP parties. The chapter analyses whether the parties in the groups worked together, and the extent to which they were actively engaged in the EP's legislative decision-making process. We then turn to the 'public face' of the groups outside parliament, by investigating through press releases whether (and how) the parties sought to use their EP alliances and fellow group members in national election campaigns. Furthermore, we analyse the patterns of public events staged by the groups and their connected 'Europarties' to see whether they actively promoted their alliances. We find that the three EP groups behaved similarly in the EP, but in markedly different ways outside it. These behaviours are in line with their strategic goals discussed in previous chapters, where the mainstream ECR parties were engaged inside the EP but not outside, the instrumental EFDD did not work together at all, and the outward-looking ENF focused on portraying unity beyond the EP. Finally, we investigate changes in groups' composition since their formation, focusing on the Sweden Democrats' July 2018 decision to leave the EFDD and join the ECR.

The concluding chapter, 'International Populism and Transnational Populism', summarises our main findings and their significance. We consider the future for radical right populists in the EP and the factors for and against the creation of a lasting, unique, ideologically homogenous radical right populist group. These include the potentially unifying effects of the post-Brexit withdrawal of the UK Conservatives and UKIP, and divisive issues such as the very diverse attitudes to Russia and Vladimir Putin found among radical right populists. Finally, we argue that, given greater public support for EU membership and the fact that the chief concern of radical right populists, namely immigration, is perceived first and foremost as a European issue, RRPs are likely in coming years to continue to mix 'international populism' and 'transnational populism', by presenting themselves not just as saviours of their nations, but of Europe.

2

# RADICAL RIGHT POPULISTS AND GROUP FORMATION IN THE EUROPEAN PARLIAMENT

The parties at the core of this book are radical right populist (RRP) parties. In this chapter, we first set out what we mean by the term 'radical right populist', before examining the history of co-operation (or the lack thereof) between RRP parties in the EP. We then discuss the main theories used to explain why parties form the groups they do in the EP, and look at how these might apply to RRP parties. Finally, we present the data and methods used in our study.

## Radical right populism

In conceptualising populism, we follow the large body of scholarship that adopts an ideational approach (Stanley 2008; Albertazzi and McDonnell 2015; Akkerman et al. 2016; Mudde 2017). In other words, we understand populism as 'first and foremost a set of ideas characterised by an antagonism between the people and the elite' (Gidron and Bonikowski 2013: 6). As Canovan (1981: 294) argues: 'all forms of populism without exception involve some kind of exaltation of and appeal to "the people" and all are in one sense or another anti-elitist'. This moral juxtaposition of a good 'people' with bad 'elites' is the basis for Mudde's widely-used definition of populism as 'a thin-centred ideology that considers society to be ultimately separated into two homogeneous and antagonistic groups, "the pure people" versus "the corrupt elite", and which argues that politics should be an expression of the *volonté générale* (general will) of the people' (Mudde 2007: 23).

Populists present themselves as the sole true defenders of the sole true people. This implies, as Jan-Werner Müller (2016: 20) argues, that 'populists are always anti-pluralist: populists claim that they, and only they, represent the people'. Within this logic, it is necessarily the populist movement itself that 'authentically identifies and represents this real or true people' (Müller 2016: 22–23). Having defined their people and elites, populists cast themselves as being on a mission to return the sovereignty usurped by those elites to its true owner, the people. As Hanspeter Kriesi (2014: 363) puts it: 'the central populist message is that politics has escaped popular control and that popular control has to be restored'. Populists therefore 'speak and behave as if democracy meant the power of the people and only the power of the people' (Mény and Surel 2002: 9). In this way, they exploit the gap between what the ideal of democracy promises (as Lincoln put it, 'government of the people, by the people, for the people') and what contemporary liberal democracies actually deliver (limited and restrained majority rule in the name of the people).

The above conceptions of 'the people' and 'elites' are common to populist movements of both right and left, but right-wing populism has some additional features. Most notably, 'the people' are said to be menaced not only from above by political, cultural, media, financial, judicial and other elites, but also from below by the presence of 'dangerous others' within society who do not share the values of the people and threaten their prosperity. Moreover, whether it concerns jobs, houses or rights, these 'others' are said to be favoured by the elites over the people. The main 'others' for right-wing populists in Western democracies have undoubtedly been immigrants (especially Muslims after 9/11), but the 'others' can be homosexuals, 'undeserving' welfare recipients, Romani communities, communist sympathisers or any group within society whose ethnic identity, religious/political beliefs or behaviour may be construed as placing them not just outside 'the people', but in an antagonistic relationship with them.

Since populism is a thin-centred ideology, we always find it alongside thick ideologies of left and right or with other thin ideologies such as nationalism (Freeden 1998; Stanley 2008). In other words, while a party may be left-wing populist, nationalist populist, regionalist populist, right-wing populist etc., it will never be just 'populist'. For the parties we focus on in this book, their thick ideology is 'radical right', and their thin ideology is 'populist'. In the past, some of these (the FN, for example) were referred to as 'extreme right' (see Arzheimer 2018). However, following Mudde (2019), we distinguish between radical right parties (i.e. those we focus upon in our study) and extreme right parties (like Golden Dawn). As Mudde explains, 'The extreme right rejects the essence of democracy, i.e. popular sovereignty and majority rule' while 'The radical right accepts the essence of democracy, but opposes fundamental elements of liberal democracy, most notably minority rights, rule of law, and separation of powers' (Mudde, 2019: forthcoming).

Contemporary radical right populist parties in Western Europe share a fundamental set of values and policies, which are particularly exemplified in their nativist, authoritarian and Eurosceptic positions (Art 2011; Vasilopoulou 2018). As Mudde (2019, forthcoming) explains, nativism 'holds that states should be inhabited exclusively by members of the native group (the nation) and that non-native (or alien) elements, whether persons or ideas, are fundamentally threatening to the homogeneous nation state'. For RRPs, the extent to which different types of non-natives are threatening varies. Notably,

Muslims are considered more threatening to native values and traditions and less willing/able to assimilate than Christian immigrants from countries like the Philippines or those of South America (McDonnell, 2006: 129). Unlike these less dangerous 'others', Muslims are said by many RRP parties to want to impose their religious values and traditions on the people as part of a surreptitious 'Islamisation' process; indeed, the PVV leader Geert Wilders has regularly affirmed that Islam is not a religion, but a political ideology, which aims to subjugate Western democracies. The nativism of radical right populists goes hand in hand with their authoritarianism, which denotes 'the belief in a strictly ordered society, in which infringements on authority are to be punished severely' (Mudde 2019, forthcoming). After all, the argument goes, heavy punishments are required to re-establish order in society and deal with threats to the people from those dangerous 'others'.

Finally, radical right populists in Western Europe have been characterised by their Eurosceptic positions since the turn of the twenty-first century.[1] Unlike their constantly hard-line, front-and-centre anti-immigration stances, their criticism of the EU and integration oscillated in strength and saliences during the years prior to the 2008 crisis (Taggart and Sczcerbiak 2008). However, in the post-global financial crisis (GFC) period, which was particularly difficult for the EU, Western European radical right populist parties were constant proponents of strong Eurosceptic positions (Vasilopoulou 2018). While some radical right populists like the Austrian Freedom Party (FPÖ), the Danish People's Party (DF) and the Italian Northern League (LN) did not go as far as UKIP, the French National Front (FN) and the Dutch Party for Freedom (PVV) in calling for exit from the EU, all of these parties sought to take advantage of the difficulties encountered by the EU by hardening their positions on European integration and/or making these more salient (McDonnell and Werner 2018b). As Pirro et al. (2018) argue, what distinguishes right-wing populists from their left-wing counterparts during the post-2008 period is that RRPs put both socio-economic and socio-cultural critiques of the EU at the centre of their framing of the issue, while left-wing populists focused predominately on socio-economic aspects. Thus, RRPs not only lamented the alleged detrimental effects of the Euro but also, as Bornschier (2011: 176) argues, made a strong sovereignty argument 'for the primacy of autonomous national politics vis-à-vis obligations arising from European integration', in addition to lamenting the alleged incompetence of bureaucrats and institutions in 'Brussels' and the culturally homogenising efforts of supranational elites (see also Vasilopoulou 2018).

There are two final points we should discuss here. The first concerns the longevity of radical right populists in Western Europe and party organisation. For many years, the prevailing wisdom among scholars was that the prominence of populist parties was destined to be episodic. Paul Taggart (2004: 270) observed that 'populist politicians, movements or parties emerge and grow quickly and gain attention but find it difficult to sustain that momentum and therefore will usually fade fast', while Canovan (2005: 89) asserted that 'populist movements tend to be spasmodic, flaring up briefly and dying away almost as fast'. However, while parties like New Democracy in 1990s Sweden, and the Dutch Pim Fortuyn List in the first decade of the twenty-first century, conformed to the 'episodic' idea, these 'flash' parties now appear more as the exceptions than the rule (Rydgren 2008; Lucardie 2008). The French FN has existed since 1972 and posted its best presidential election result to date in 2017; the Lega Nord is the oldest party in the Italian parliament and not only returned to government in 2018, but did so on the back of its highest ever share of the vote. The Austrian Freedom Party recovered from both a party split and a very unhappy experience in government at the beginning of the 2000s to bounce back in subsequent elections and once more formed a coalition with the centre-right in 2017.

Moreover, parties like the Danish People's Party, the Lega Nord and the Front National have all survived the passage of 'charismatic' founder-leaders in the last decade and gone on to greater electoral success. So, while Geert Wilders' PVV in the Netherlands may be a personal party akin to those founded by Silvio Berlusconi, in which the party lifespan is tied to the leader's political career, it is not typical of populist party organisations in Western Europe (de Lange and Art 2011; Kefford and McDonnell 2018). On the contrary, as Heinisch and Mazzoleni (2016: 238) conclude at the end of their edited collection on European radical right populist party organisation, 'all the parties in our sample not only fulfil Janda's criteria for institutionalization but have continued moving toward organizational "normality"'.

Most successful radical right populist parties in Europe today have established deep roots and structures that are built to last. That said, they do have a greater tendency than other parties to be dominated by their leaders and to personalise communications around them. As Heinsich and Mazzoleni (2016: 239–40) explain, they differ from mainstream parties as regards the degree of 'centralisation of power in the leadership'. This, as we will see, especially in Chapter 5, can make it easier for radical right populist leaders to enact major shifts on policies and strategies quickly, unhindered by internal consultations.

The second, and final, point concerns radical right populists in power. Not only have they continued to grow electorally and created solid party organisations, but one of the major changes for RRPs in the twenty-first century has been that they have increasingly become acceptable partners for mainstream parties in government, whether by providing parliamentary support for centre-right administrations as on several occasions in Denmark, or by joining the major centre-right party in cabinet, as the FPÖ have done in Austria. Certainly, the furore—and sanctions—from Austria's fourteen EU partners that met the FPÖ's entry into coalition in 2000 were unthinkable when the same coalition formed in 2017. Moreover, Albertazzi and McDonnell (2015) show that populists are by no means doomed to failure in office, as many scholars previously predicted.[2] Rather, parties like the Lega Nord and the Swiss People's Party have shown that they can achieve success on key policies (for example, regarding asylum seekers or by introducing tougher laws on crime), while compromising on others, all without suffering party splits and vote losses of the type experienced by the FPÖ in the early 2000s.

## Radical right populists in the European Parliament

One of the ironies for radical right populists in Western Europe in recent decades is that, while they decry wasteful EU institutions, the EP has been the main representative arena, and an important source of funding, for some of them. The domestic electoral systems in France and the UK, with their strong majoritarian elements, have long kept both the FN and UKIP out of national parliament, or left them with very few representatives. Indeed, UKIP's only MPs in the House of Commons have been two former Conservative parliamentarians who switched to UKIP in 2014, but left again in 2015 and 2017. While other radical right populist parties are present in their national legislatures, several are rendered largely insignificant because other parties apply *cordons sanitaires* (i.e. agreements not to enter into any kind of election or governing deals with RRPs). The FN, the Flemish VB and the Sweden Democrats have faced this situation consistently, while the Dutch PVV and the Austrian Freedom Party have spent much of their existence living under *cordons sanitaires*, even if they have also had periods in which they have provided parliamentary support for, or been part of, the national government. In short, while things are clearly changing in the current decade regarding their acceptability as mainstream partners, radical right populists have spent much of their domestic history as pariahs.

One might imagine, therefore, that the European level has provided an opportunity for RRPs to gain respite from their domestic isolation and work alongside other likeminded parties in the EP. Yet, despite seemingly ample common ground in terms of ideology and policy, co-operation between European radical right populists has been far more limited than that seen in other party families. As we noted in the previous chapter, parties elected to the EP tend to sit in long-standing groups with those parties from other countries that most closely resemble them ideologically. Hence, the German Christian Democrats are in the European People's Party

(EPP) alongside other centre-right parties such as the Spanish People's Party and the Swedish Moderate Party. Likewise, we find the Italian Democratic Party and the German Social Democrats allied with centre-left parties from across Europe in the Party of European Socialists (PES), while those further to the left are together in the European United Left/Nordic Green Left (GUE/NGL).[3] Indeed, the long-standing unity of the radical left GUE/NGL group presents an interesting contrast to the long-standing division of the radical right. Created in 1995, GUE/NGL has been present ever since and, alongside more recent members like Syriza from Greece and Podemos from Spain, the group has contained MEPs from radical left populist parties such as the Dutch Socialist Party (1999–2019) and the Irish Sinn Féin (since 2004).

Radical right populists enjoy no such history of unity. The FN did succeed in leading small groups in the 1984–1989 and 1989–1994 parliaments, on the first occasion with the Movimento Sociale Italiano (MSI—Italian Social Movement) and the Greek National Political Union (EPEN), and on the second with the German Republikaner and the predecessor of the Flemish Vlaams Belang, the Vlaams Blok (VB—Flemish Blok). However, the FN was only able to put together two other (fleeting) groups prior to the 2014–2019 parliament. First, the Technical Group of Independents in 1999 which contained the FN, Lega and VB, but also the libertarian

Bonino List from Italy. After a long investigation and dispute, this was ultimately disbanded in 2001 by the EP due to its lack of a common policy profile (Hix et al. 2005; see our explanation of EP rules for groups later in this chapter). Second, in the 2004–09 parliament, the FN led the creation of the 'Identity, Tradition and Sovereignty' group. This contained the FN, VB and FPÖ, along with a collection of far-right MEPs from Western and Eastern Europe, and lasted only from January to November 2007 before splitting (Almeida, 2010; Startin, 2010). The FN would spend the next seven and a half years without a group affiliation.

Table 2.1: The main radical right populist parties of ECR, EFDD and ENF since 1999

|      | DF  | PS | SD   | UKIP    | LN       | FN | VB | FPÖ | PVV |
|------|-----|----|------|---------|----------|----|----|-----|-----|
| 1999 | UEN |    |      | EDD     | TGI & NI |    |    | NI  |     |
| 2004 |     |    |      | IND/DEM | UEN      | *  | *  | *   |     |
| 2009 | EFD |    |      | EFD     |          |    |    |     |     |
| 2015 | ECR |    | EFDD |         | ENF      |    |    |     |     |

Notes: UEN = Union for Europe of the Nations, EDD = Europe of Democracies and Diversities, IND/DEM = Independents/Democrats, TGI = Technical Group of Independents (formed in 1999, dissolved in 2001), NI = Non-Inscrits (Non-aligned), EFD = Europe of Freedom and Democracy, ECR = Europe of Conservatives and Reformists, EFDD = Europe of Freedom and Direct Democracy, ENF = Europe of Nations and Freedom. Parties not in the EP are shaded in grey.

* FN, FPÖ and VB were part of the group 'Identity, Tradition, Sovereignty' from January to November 2007.

As we can see from Table 2.1, other Western European radical right populist parties have either not been in the EP for much of the last two decades—like the Sweden Democrats, Finns Party (PS) and the Dutch PVV—or they have moved regularly from one short-lived and often not particularly congruent group to another (like UKIP, Lega Nord and the Danish People's Party). Alternatively, like FN, they have spent much of their time among the non-inscrits (this is true, in particular, of the VB and FPÖ). In short, none have been part of a long-standing ideologically homogenous radical right populist group. Certainly, there is no radical right equivalent of the radical left GUE/NGL. In the fifteen years between 1999 and 2014, the nine parties we focus on in this book were part of no fewer than ten different groups, or were non-aligned.

There has been a mixture of reasons for this history of division, including conflicting national interests, conflicting types of nationalism, tensions between nationalities and fears about being tainted by association with one another (Fieschi 2000; Minkenberg and Perrineau 2007; Startin 2010). Almost two decades ago, Fieschi (2000: 518) argued: 'the difficulties encountered in attempts to form parliamentary groups are indicative of the primacy of nationalisms which undermine any potential for ideological alliances'. Tensions have occurred, for example, over contested borders and the minority communities left on either side of them.

Notably, the status and rights of the German-speaking population in the Italian-controlled Alto Adige/Südtirol continues to be a recurring source of disagreement between radical right Austrians and Italians.[4] Another source of division has been the different natures of RRP nationalisms, principally between ethnic nationalists such as the VB (whose people are the Flemish, not the Belgians) or the LN (whose 'people' until a few years ago were simply northern Italians, not all Italians) and state nationalists such as FN, for whom the idea of nation-states in Europe being divisible in the ways proposed by LN and VB was anathema (Mudde 2007: 167–68). Tensions have also risen when one radical right populist casts another's people as 'dangerous others'. For example, the Italian MEP Alessandra Mussolini's comments in November 2007 about Romanians being criminals prompted the Romanian MEPs from the Identity, Tradition and Sovereignty group to leave, causing its collapse.[5]

The former FN leader Jean-Marie Le Pen and another prominent FN MEP, Bruno Gollnisch, tried periodically to overcome these national (and nationalist) differences between radical right populists and achieve what Fieschi (2000: 521) termed 'the reconciliation of attitudes through the concept of a Europe of the fatherlands'. We can see that sentiment explicitly, for example, in the statement on the (now defunct) webpage of the (also now defunct) loosely organised European National

Union (ENU—known as 'Euronat') launched by FN in 1997: 'The Nationalist phenomenon cannot be and will not be restricted to an island, co-operation is essential to achieve freedom and our common goals' (cited in Startin 2010: 437). Similar transnational principles underpinned the Identity, Tradition and Sovereignty group. As Startin (2010: 438) argued, the idea of a shared Christian European identity and values system being under threat, acted 'as a motivating factor with regard to the rationale behind the group's formation, certainly among the main protagonists from Austria, Belgium and France', i.e. the FPÖ, VB and FN.

The obstacles inherent in creating an 'international group of nationalists' discussed above have been compounded by the perceived domestic reputational risks of European-level co-operation for radical right populists, especially those seeking to moderate their image at the national level and/or enter national governments via coalitions. Fieschi (2000) and Startin (2010) note how the FPÖ avoided relationships with other RRP parties such as the Front National in the late 1990s when it wanted to be accepted by the Austrian centre-right as a potential governing partner. We can see the same dynamic at work, particularly vis-à-vis Front National, for other radical right populist parties that have either been in government, or were seeking co-operation with mainstream parties. For example, the founder-leader of the Lega Nord, Umberto Bossi (at the time a minister in the Berlusconi-led Italian coalition government), declared in 2002: 'We are the opposite of Le Pen and anyone who compares us is a lowlife' (*Corriere della Sera* 2002). Similarly, Geert Wilders, whose PVV would subsequently prop up a minority centre-right government in the Netherlands from 2010 to 2012 in exchange for policy concessions, stated in 2008: 'My allies are not Le Pen or Haider' (*The Guardian* 2008). Discussing why some European radical right populists shunned others in the last decade, Almeida (2010: 246–47) concluded that radical right co-operation at the European level is

> ... a strategy [that] implies a public disclosure of affinities with other radical right parties. While membership in a radical right political group opens the possibility to frame policy preferences in a European context and to maximise resources and visibility in the EP, it represents a costly strategy in terms of domestic legitimacy.

## *Theories of EP group formation*

In this section, we set out our theoretical framework, which follows the classic coalition theory trifecta of 'policy, office or votes'. Before doing so, it is important to highlight a series of pre-conditions for group formation in the EP that are specific to this particular environment.

While the rules have changed over time as the EU (and therefore the EP) enlarged, a group in the 2009–2014 parliament had to comprise at least twenty-five

MEPs from at least one-quarter of the member states (seven, in 2014) and these MEPs had to share 'political affinities' (Rules of Procedure of the EP 2009: Rule 30). The provision of shared 'political affinities' was designed to prevent MEPs with very different programmes from forming pragmatic alliances, simply to access the spoils of group formation (such as the Technical Group of Independents in 1999, mentioned above). Thus, before any other theoretical explanation for group formation becomes relevant, these numerical hurdles must be taken into consideration by parties aspiring to form a group.

## The framework: Policy, office and votes

How can we explain the EP alliance behaviour of radical right populist parties? Scholars analysing EP group formation processes have adapted the framework developed by Wolfgang C. Müller and Kaare Strøm (1990) to distinguish the policy, office and vote-seeking motivations behind coalition formations at national level. The national level mechanisms focus on the main types of motivation that inform the behaviour of political parties, particularly when weighing up their coalition options. They are ideal types that can be combined and often reinforce each other (Müller and Strøm 1990: 8). The first motivation, according to this framework, pertains to office-seeking parties that primarily aim to maximise their control over public office and the advantages that holding such office brings (Müller and Strøm 1990: 6). Meanwhile, Müller and Strøm argue that the underlying and ultimate reasons for seeking office might vary, including intrinsic and instrumental logics (1990: 6–7), thus such parties will prioritise their ambition of entering government over other considerations. Consequently they will usually form a national government whenever they can.

The second motivational logic is that of the policy-seeking party, which primarily focuses on influencing the policy making of the government. While this party also seeks to control the government, it does so for the purpose of putting its policy program into action. Thus, the party will only form coalitions with other parties if this facilitates enacting their preferred policies, or as Müller and Strøm put it: 'Policy-based coalition theory … assumes that coalitions are made by parties that are congenial in policy terms.' (1990: 7).

The third and final motivation refers to vote-seeking parties that, as the name suggests, aim to maximise the number of votes they receive at elections. This motivation primarily influences parties' behaviour in terms of the policy positions they take before the election (Müller and Strøm 1990: 8–9), but is necessarily instrumental, as maximising votes could either be aimed at office or policy. However, a pure vote-seeking rationale can come into play with regards to coalition building, when parties try to predict the effect of government participation on future election outcomes. If forming a coalition is seen as too risky for the electoral fortunes of the party in the long run, it might lead parties to pass up the opportunity to enter government at that point (Müller and Strøm 1990: 9).

This framework was obviously not created for the alliance logics within the European Parliament. Notably, the parties and groups in the EP do not create a 'European government', as the two executive organs (the European Council and the European Commission) are formed independently of the EP. However, the framework is still applicable because the EP, at a basic level, consists of MEPs grouped in national parties. Relative to the size of the whole parliament, these parties are small and would not be effective by themselves. Thus, national parties form larger groups, which act together to develop and vote on European legislation. Thus, even though the parties in the EP do not form a government, they participate in a coalition-building process to form EP groups. The framework of policy, office and vote can therefore be applied to these processes, even though the specific mechanisms are necessarily different from those at the national level.

Policy: Congruence leads to group formation

As we have seen, the dominant theoretical explanation for parties' formation of groups in the EP has been policy congruence. McElroy and Benoit (2010, 2011) show that EP groups usually have two main characteristics. First, they are internally cohesive in their policy positions, meaning that parties from different countries with similar ideological profiles band together. Secondly, when comparing these groups, McElroy and Benoit find that they are distinct from each other, meaning that there is no significant ideological overlap. There are exceptions of course, but, overall, 'policy congruence is far and away the single most important driving factor guiding national parties in their decisions to join transnational party groups' (McElroy and Benoit 2010: 397). Bressanelli (2012) and Whitaker and Lynch (2014), who each use different data and analysis methods to McElroy and Benoit, come to similar conclusions for the group alliances adopted by Western European parties after the 2009 EP elections. Likewise, Maurer et al. (2008: 251–2) find that, in most cases, 'parties will choose to join the largest group that broadly shares its socioeconomic preferences'. The logic of this policy congruence is similar to that of national parties forming: likeminded MEPs (and parties) work together to further the interests of their constituency by following a broad shared ideological program.

## Office: chasing EP spoils

While the above studies agree that policy congruence is the key driver of alliances, 'office' can also be a strong motivation for wanting to join a group. Although parties cannot win governmental participation at EU level, the most influential positions within the EP (chairs and rapporteurs) are allocated through the parliamentary groups. These are among a range of advantages that group membership brings, along with greater speaking time in the parliament, staffing and funding (Settembri 2004). The desire to access these spoils has played a significant role in the creation of several groups that include radical right populists. It was undoubtedly the driver of the Technical Group of Independents, which was formed in 1999 and ultimately disbanded by the EP for lack of a common policy profile (Hix et al. 2005). And, while it was not the only factor, office played a strong role in the short-lived Independence, Tradition and Sovereignty group (Startin 2010). Whitaker and Lynch (2014: 258) discuss how UKIP's decision to form the EFD in 2009 was primarily motivated by its need to secure these resources and publicity (see Chapter 4). Fitzgibbon and Leruth (2017: 167) concur, arguing that what co-operation there has been between right-wing Eurosceptic parties in the EP has generally been based 'on purely strategic and utilitarian concerns. Right-wingers wanted the resources that forming an EP group provided'.

The degree to which office can play a role in the EP merits closer inspection. In general, the spoils of group formation itself are unchanged, as the rule book of the

EP has not been fundamentally altered in recent decades. However, two aspects of the rules might influence a party's preference for group membership. First, from an office perspective, group membership is generally preferable to being unaffiliated (non-inscrits, in EP-speak). While non-inscrits might be part of a national party, their lack of affiliation to an EP group means that they do not enjoy any of the opportunities available to EP groups, such as leading legislative positions in the EP committee system. Although non-inscrit MEPs receive individual funding from the EP budget, their financial resources are markedly smaller than those of MEPs that are part of groups with much larger budgets. Similarly, their parliamentary speaking time is restricted to their own allocated time. By contrast, group members can be allocated a broader range of time slots depending on the intra-group procedure used to assign these. In sum, all things being equal, a rational MEP and their party would prefer membership of a group over being in the Non-Inscrits.

Beyond the formation of a group in order to access EP spoils, Bressanelli (2012) finds that resource and office attribution can also influence a party's decision regarding which specific EP group to join. In particular, he shows a relationship between the size of the individual party and the group, with larger parties opting for the larger and more influential EP groups (2012: 747). Thus, the second aspect of the EP rules that potentially influences party preferences regarding groups is the fact that larger groups get more resources. The larger the group, the more money they receive from the EP and the more speaking time is allocated to the group (EP Rules of Procedure, article 162). The increase in these resources is approximately linear to the number of MEPs and the amount of different countries represented in the group (Bressanelli and de Candia 2018: 7). The votes in a key organisational organ in the EP, the Conference of Presidents, are also weighted by the number of MEPs in a group. Furthermore, larger groups are better placed to get their members elected to the chairmanship of EP committees. When allocating these offices, the EP uses the D'Hondt method, which is proportional but rewards larger parties (Bressanelli and de Candia 2018: 6). Similarly, larger groups receive more 'points', which they can then use to bid for rapporteur positions on EP committees.

On the other hand, membership of larger groups does have disadvantages, in that the influence of individual MEPs and their national parties is logically smaller, the more MEPs and other parties are also in the group. Larger groups mean more internal competition for positions, whether within the parliament or within the group itself (for example, co-chair roles). While we would generally assume MEPs to prefer larger over smaller groups for their greater office spoils, there is likely a mechanism of diminishing returns.

## Votes: EP alliances for national motives

Scholars have considered national vote-seeking motivations much less likely to influence EP group formation. This is largely because EP elections are widely viewed as second-order elections (Reif and Schmitt 1980), at which voters and the general public ascribe less relevance to the outcomes compared to general (national) elections.

This perceived lack of relevance has a range of consequences for voter behaviour and election results, including lower voter turnout, better chances of success for smaller and newer parties (since voters are more willing to experiment and/or follow their true party preferences) and worse outcomes for national government parties because voters are more prepared to express their dissatisfaction without expecting negative consequences (Reif and Schmitt 1980: 9–10). The theory implies that the dominant level—that is, the national level—and its concerns and reasoning determine the decision-making processes of voters in second-order elections. We know that parties react to this by devoting fewer resources to EP election campaigns and focusing these campaigns on national matters (Brunsbach et al. 2012). Maurer et al. (2008: 249) argue that vote-seeking behaviour with a specific view on the European level might be possible if the issues at hand are salient among voters and if voters are aware of their party's behaviour at the EP level, but they suggest that this is rare.

Nonetheless, there are reasons why radical right populist parties might consider the potential reactions of national electorates and elites when making European-level alliances. For example, as mentioned previously, the FN, VB and SD have long faced a situation whereby mainstream parties in their national party systems refuse *a priori* to consider co-operation with them. If such a party had the removal of this *cordon sanitaire* as a strategic goal, then the legitimation granted by an EP alliance, especially with non-radical parties, could help them. More broadly, entry into certain groups might be seen as providing a 'reputational shield' for radical parties against accusations of extremism (Ivarsflaten 2006). While for Ivarsflaten, party history—for example, as an agrarian party—can help anti-immigration parties fend off hostile elites and help voters justify their party choice (2006: 6–7), joining a group with established mainstream parties might provide a similar reputational shield for radical right populists. This was the case for the post-Fascist Alleanza Nazionale (AN—National Alliance) party in Italy, which explicitly set acceptance into the European People's Party (EPP) as a strategic goal on its journey to greater public respectability in the 2000s (Tarchi 2013: 704).[6] Fieschi (2000: 524) observes that AN's desire for 'respectability' also meant that, unlike its predecessor the MSI, it refused to be associated with parties such as Front National in the 1990s. Similarly, as we noted earlier, the Austrian Freedom

Party (FPÖ) initially avoided allying with other radical right parties in the EP in order to be more acceptable as a coalition partner for the Austrian centre-right after the 1999 general election. While the Austrian case was very unusual at the time, Western European RRP parties now increasingly aspire to be 'coalitionable' and therefore wish to be seen by national publics and both media and political elites as acceptable partners for mainstream centre-right parties. Consequently, we should not exclude the possibility that domestic goals such as extending their electoral appeal, removing a *cordon sanitaire* and/or acquiring 'coalitionability' might influence contemporary radical right populist EP alliance strategies. This may be particularly relevant when—as was the case for UKIP, SD, PS and the DF in 2014—parties are facing a general election in the year after the EP elections (i.e. when their group choice may still be recent news).

## *Our data*

In order to investigate whether, and to what extent, the above theories explain the alliance strategies of radical right populists in the 2014–2019 EP, and to uncover alternative explanations, we rely on a series of established and unique data. To test the 'policy' explanation, we examine the positional congruence of the ECR, EFDD and ENF using party position data provided by the Chapel Hill Expert Survey (CHES) (Bakker et al.

2015). For the 'office' explanations, we collected information about the groups' EP funding and parliamentary positions from the European Parliament's webpages. For the role of 'votes', and in order to investigate whether other explanations outside the 'policy, office, votes' framework are relevant, we rely on our interviews with current and former party representatives and officials in all nine RRP parties and their main non-RRP partners (where relevant). We augment this data through information collected from the EP webpage, the national party webpages and newspaper reports.

Since the main established theory to explain EP group formation is based on the positional congruence of the national parties, we establish the internal positional fit for each of the ECR, EFDD and ENF groups, compare them to one another and to hypothetical alternative groups containing all RRP parties. As the defining policy positions of Western European radical right populist parties are their anti-immigration and Eurosceptic positions, these dimensions are central to our investigation. We also investigate the group congruence on the socio-economic left–right dimension, meaning the conflict over the degree of economic regulation and the extent of the welfare state, as well as the social left–right dimension, meaning the conflict between traditional, authoritarian vs liberal, post-material views of society. To place the parties along these dimensions, we use the Chapel Hill Expert Survey (CHES) data that was collected in the run-up to the 2009 and 2014 European Parliament elections (Bakker et al. 2015; Polk et al. 2017). CHES surveys party experts in all included countries, and asks them to place the national parties on policy dimensions by allocating pre-defined numerical values, including on EU-related policies as well as a range of economic and social value policies. Multiple experts are asked to place the same parties and the average placement is deemed to be the party position. There is a broad methodological debate about the advantages and disadvantages of different approaches to measuring party positions. Within these debates, the CHES data has been used widely and its reliability and validity have been established numerous times (Hooghe et al. 2010; Marks et al. 2007; Netjes and Binnema 2007; Volkens 2007).

We use the CHES instead of other party position data for a number of reasons. In general, all sources of party positions have advantages and disadvantages and the CHES data is no exception to this rule. The main issue with expert surveys is that it is not totally clear which element of the party an individual expert assesses. National and European election manifestos, leader speeches, parliamentary behaviour along with media reporting and general shared knowledge might contribute to evaluation of this general 'party position'. Therefore, we will discuss any unexpected party positions that we encounter in the next three chapters. And, since CHES surveys multiple experts per party and averages their evaluations, this should lead to party positions being relatively unaffected by any specific aspect the experts focus on, as long as the party is not internally extremely heterogeneous.

Other sources of party positions are based only on the election manifestos, either for national elections (Budge et al. 2001; Volkens et al. 2018; Werner et al. 2014) or for European elections (Schmitt et al. 2018). The advantage of the manifesto approach is the clarity of what is measured, as these positions are based only on the text created by the party for a specific election. However, the text analysis approach used by the Manifesto and Euromanifesto projects has come in for a lot of criticism (e.g. Gemenis 2013). Furthermore, general election manifestos are not helpful for our purposes as these are created for a specific general election, which does not coincide with the European election. However, using the manifestos produced for the EP elections is problematic because they are unlikely to be primarily about the EP election and European issues. As discussed earlier, elections to the European Parliament are widely considered second-order elections (Reif and Schmitt 1980; Brunsbach et al. 2012). Thus, it is not clear whether the content of Euromanifestos is a true reflection of the parties' positions.[7] In summary, while there are various sources available from which to establish party positions, we use the CHES data because it provides us with direct measures of the positions and saliences that are most relevant for radical right populist parties. Keeping the limitations of this data in mind, we will be critical in assessing these positions and point to instances where they hide more complex policy profiles.

To investigate whether joining specific groups has had financial or other office-related advantages for individual parties, we collected a range of information from the European Parliament's website.[8] This provides information for all current and past MEPs, about their party and group affiliations, group leadership positions (such as group chairs and vice-chairs), EP committee membership and leadership, as well as rapporteur, positions. We recorded the number of such positions for all MEPs in our nine RRP parties and their main non-RRP group members for the 2009–2014 and 2014–2019 EP parliaments. This data source also allowed us to trace the movement of MEPs between groups and any changes in party affiliations during the legislature. Furthermore, all EP groups are required to report on their income and spending to the EP administration, which makes these audit reports available to the public.[9] Owing to long reporting time frames, the group reports for 2017 are the most recent available at the time of writing, while the last audit report for the non-inscrits is from 2015.

We complement the party position and office data with information gathered through semi-structured interviews with a total of thirty-one current and former MEPs, national MPs and officials at various levels of the parties in the ECR, EFDD and ENF. These comprised not only interviewees from the nine radical right populist parties that we focus on, but also key representatives from their main non-radical right partners, such as the UK Conservatives and the Italian M5S (see the appendix for a full list). These interviews are also the basis for the alternative explanations that we offer. We conducted a first round of interviews in Brussels, Strasbourg, Stockholm, Vienna and Milan in June–July 2014 in the immediate aftermath of the EP elections and the formation of the ECR and EFDD groups (and the failure of the future ENF parties to form a group). A second round of interviews took place in June 2015 in Brussels and Strasbourg when the ENF group was finally created. Third, fourth and fifth rounds were conducted in Brussels and Stockholm (May 2017), Copenhagen (March 2018), and London and Paris (October-November 2018). We spoke to several interviewees on different occasions during the 2014–2018 period.

Our interviewees were all figures who could shed light on the logics underpinning their parties' alliance strategies and actions at European level. In other words, we did not simply interview party elites and hope they might be useful. Rather, we interviewed people whom we knew—whether from media reports or other interviewees—had been involved in the decisions and negotiations leading to their party's EP group choice. For some parties these were MEPs, for others they were leading national representatives or party officials, and for some we needed to speak to a mixture. For example, to understand why the Danish People's Party and Finns Party were not accepted into the ECR in 2009, but were admitted in 2014, we needed to talk to the Conservative MEPs Geoffrey van Orden and Dan Hannan, whom we knew had played important roles in these events. Similarly, we were aware from other interviewees (both inside and outside his party) that we had to speak to the Danish People's Party MEP Morten Messerschmidt, since he was given a relatively free hand by the party leadership back home to determine and negotiate their EP alliances (see Chapter 3). In contrast, we learned very quickly that the key people from the Sweden Democrats who, in 2014, were discussing and deciding such matters were not the party's two MEPs, but its international secretary Kent Ekeroth and a handful of leading MPs, including Richard Jomshof (see Chapter 4).

Interviewees were asked to discuss the evolution of their parties' positions on the EU and European integration, how they had constructed alliances at EP level in the past and present, the logics and processes that had led to these, along with their views on the desirability of other parties as partners. All interviewees agreed to be recorded and all, with the exception of one high-ranking UKIP official and one official from the Austrian Freedom Party, agreed to be named. Interviews were conducted in

English, French and Italian. Eight of the nine radical right populist parties from the ECR, EFDD and ENF groups were happy to talk to us. The only exception was the Dutch PVV, which is known for refusing to speak to academics (thankfully, their former MEP Lucas Hartong was willing to drive from Amsterdam to Brussels to be interviewed at length). Otherwise, we found that leading figures from parties like the Front National, Vlaams Belang and the Danish People's Party were extremely generous with their time. Rather than being hostile to academic research, as some might expect, they were as willing to engage and speak openly as politicians we have interviewed from mainstream parties and, in some cases, much more so. This augurs well for future research on radical right populists.

Finally, we rely on a range of sources in Chapter 6, where we investigate the roles these groups play for individual MEPs and, especially, the national parties. We use VoteWatch data (votewatch.eu), which collates MEPs' voting records, to investigate whether radical right populists vote with one another and/or their group members within the EP. To explore how and to what extent radical right populist parties use their EP group membership as a tool during national election campaigns, we analysed press releases and, where possible, news items gathered from the parties' webpages. We collected these press releases for the six-month period before the national elections that have taken place in

Austria, Finland, France, Italy, the Netherlands, and Sweden since the 2014 EP election, and analysed them qualitatively.

*Conclusion*

When the 2014 European election results came in, mainstream politicians and media commentators spoke of a 'populist earthquake'.[10] While this was overstated, given that high-profile parties such as the PVV, VB and LN all fared worse than they had in 2009, it was true that the total number of radical right populist MEPs was higher than ever, at seventy-three out of 751. Moreover, in France, the UK and Denmark, radical right populist parties topped the polls for the first time.

Yet, if we look at what happened afterwards, once the media furore had died down, we find that those three 'big winners' on the radical right, the Danish People's Party, UKIP and Front National, all ended up in different EP groups: the ECR, EFDD and ENF. As we have discussed in this chapter, that outcome is puzzling at first glance. Radical right populists like the winning (and losing) parties in 2014 share similar ideological features, in particular their populist conceptions of 'the people', 'elites' and 'others', which complement their radical right nativist and authoritarian views. Notably, they combine anti-immigrant policies with varying degrees of Euroscepticism. According to the main political science literature on EP group formation, their presumed policy congruence should bring them together. Yet, they have long been the 'odd ones out' in the EP, where they have never established the type of long-standing broad alliance seen on the centre-right, centre-left and radical left. We have discussed some of the reasons in this chapter: conflicting nationalist agendas, conflicting forms of nationalism, and fears of being tainted by association (especially with the Front National). We do not know to what extent these remained relevant in the 2014–2019 parliament. Certainly, neither those factors nor considerations of policy congruence seem to explain the Danish People's Party and Finns Party leaving UKIP's group to join the ECR, led by the UK Conservatives. But they also do not appear to explain the timing of the new-found unity on the radical right, as expressed by FN's group, the ENF. If, as we noted earlier, parties like the FN were previously policy congruent, but toxic, for the PVV and LN, what changed? And how do we account for a former extreme right party like the Sweden Democrats joining UKIP's group rather than that of the FN? Why would UKIP accept the Swedes if it shunned the FN? In the next three chapters, we will therefore focus on each of these groups individually, in order to identify and explain the logics behind their formation.

3

# EUROPEAN CONSERVATIVES AND REFORMISTS

## A VERY RESPECTABLE MARRIAGE

While the European Conservatives and Reformists (ECR) group was formally created in 2009, its roots lie in the conflicts over the previous two decades within the UK Conservatives, regarding the party's positions on Europe. In particular, we can trace the group's genesis to David Cameron's decision during the Conservative leadership battle in 2005 to match the promise by one of his rivals, Liam Fox, that the Conservatives would leave the EPP-ED group in the EP and set up a new group, which would appeal to 'pro-market, anti-integrationist and Atlanticist' centre-right MEPs (Bale 2006: 393). In the years after Cameron's election as leader, the Conservative MEP Geoffrey van Orden and Mark Francois, shadow Europe minister for the Conservatives, seized on this commitment and began the work of building a new group, but without involving the party's generally more Europhile EP delegation (interview with van Orden 2015).

This culminated in the Prague Declaration of March 2009, which set out the group's key principles.[1] It was signed in March 2009 by the three main parties that would form the ECR after that year's European elections: the UK Conservatives, the Polish Prawo i Sprawiedliwość (PiS—Law and Justice) and the Czech Občanská Demokratická Strana (ODS—Civic Democratic Party). The ODS had been alongside the Conservatives in the EPP-ED group, while PiS had previously sat in the Union for Europe of the Nations (UEN) group. The latter was a mixed ideological group containing Europhile centre-right and conservative parties alongside Eurosceptic right-wing populists such as the Dansk Folkeparti (DF—Danish People's Party) and the Italian Lega Nord (LN—Northern League) (Leruth 2018: 388). The ECR was also avowedly critical of integration, although its stated mission was to reform, not reject, the EU. The Prague Declaration, therefore, begins by talking about the urgent need to reform the EU on the basis of 'Eurorealism, openness, accountability and democracy'. While the group itself insisted that the correct term to describe it is 'Eurorealist' rather than 'Eurosceptic' (Leruth 2017: 50–51), it has usually been considered a moderate 'soft Eurosceptic' group that was more respectable and active in parliament than the EFD (Usherwood and Startin 2013; Whitaker and Lynch 2014; Leruth 2017).

The ECR's creation established a new pole of attraction for right-wing Eurosceptic parties in the EP, including some on the radical right. In particular, the group was immediately appealing to both the Danish People's Party and the Finnish Perussuomalaiset (PS—Finns Party). However, the UK Conservatives were wary of bringing in parties whose reputations might damage their own and so the two Nordic parties found a home in the UK Independence Party (UKIP)-led EFD group, instead.[2] In 2009, the Conservatives preferred quality (in terms of moderate ideological credentials and reputation) over quantity. With fifty-four MEPs from eight different member states, the ECR in 2009 had just one country more than the threshold required to form a group, and contained only three parties with more than a single MEP (the Conservatives, PiS and ODS). Notwithstanding the institutional incentives for the ECR to raise these low numbers in the next parliament, Whitaker and Lynch (2014: 259) wrote that 'its chances of growing substantially would appear to be slim'. This was, they argued, because the ECR's positions on European integration made it unlikely to attract new members from the largely centre-right European People's Party (EPP) or the Alliance of Liberals and Democrats for Europe (ALDE).

Table 3.1: Main Members of ECR, 2014

| Party | Country | Vote in 2014 | MEPs 2014 | Previous EP group |
|---|---|---|---|---|
| Conservatives | UK | 23.3 | 20 | ECR |
| PiS | Poland | 31.8 | 19 | ECR |
| AfD | Germany | 7.1 | 7 | – |
| DF | Denmark | 26.6 | 4 | EFD |
| N-VA | Belgium | 16.8 | 4 | Greens/EFA |
| PS | Finland | 12.9 | 2 | EFD |
| BWC-VRMO | Bulgaria | 10.7 | 2 | – |
| ODS | Czechia | 7.7 | 2 | ECR |
| CU-SGP | Netherlands | 7.7 | 2 | ECR (CU)/EFD (SGP) |

Notes: Votes in percentages. Number of MEPs at first session of the new EP in 2014. We only include parties with at least two MEPs. The ECR also contained individual MEPs from Ireland, Greece, Croatia, Germany, Latvia, Lithuania and Slovakia, bringing their overall number to seventy.
Source: http://www.europarl.europa.eu/elections2014-results/en/election-results-2014.html

However, the ECR in 2014 would attract—and open itself up to—two new radical right populist members coming from the EFD, namely the Danish People's Party and the Finns Party. It also brought in non-radical right members from a range of other countries, including the then ordoliberal German Alternative für Deutschland (AfD—Alternative for Germany), which would only later transform into a radical right party. The ECR started out as a group containing seventy members from fifteen different member states at the opening session of the new EP in July 2014 (see Table 3.1). This made it the third-largest group in the EP, narrowly surpassing ALDE.

In this chapter, we answer the following questions concerning the ECR's radical right populists: (1) Why did the group turn down the Danish People's Party (DF) and Finns Party (PS) in 2009, but then accept them in 2014? (2) Why did the Danes and the Finns want to join the ECR in 2014, given that their fellow radical right populists from UKIP should have provided a better ideological fit than the Conservatives? (3) At a time when parties like the Front National and Dutch Party for Freedom were seeking to establish an ideologically homogenous radical right populist EP group, why did the Danish People's Party and Finns Party not consider joining forces with them?

In line with our approach set out earlier, we first establish the policy position fit between the two radical right populist parties—DF and PS—and the three core parties of the ECR, the Conservatives, PiS and ODS. We then consider the possible office benefits for the Danes and Finns of moving groups. We find that neither 'policy' nor 'office' can fully explain the Danish People's Party and Finns Party's move from the EFD to the ECR, or the ECR's willingness to accept them. We therefore examine the material from interviews (including repeated discussions with some individuals) that we conducted between July 2014 and March 2018 with nine leading DF, PS, UK Conservative, PiS and AfD MEPs and officials who had direct knowledge of the processes around the ECR's creation and composition in 2009 and 2014, in particular concerning the attempts of the DF and PS to join.[3] Based on this, we show that the perceived domestic costs and benefits of association played a key role both in the Conservatives' decision not to admit the Nordic populists in 2009, but also in the decisions of the latter to leave the EFD, avoid other radical right populists and join the ECR in 2014. In the final section, we build on this discussion to propose our theory of 'the respectable marriage', which sees radical parties forsake policy congruence at the European level for perceived reputational benefits at home.

## *The ECR: a group of two ideological camps*

In 2009 the ECR chose not to admit the Danish People's Party and the Finns Party, but then reversed this decision in 2014. Following the dominant theory of EP group formation being based on policy congruence, this would imply that either (1) the main ECR parties (Conservatives, ODS and PiS) changed their positions on key issues between 2009 and 2014 and, in so doing, became closer to the DF and PS; (2) the DF and PS moved closer to the main ECR parties over that time or (3) all five parties moved in each other's directions. Similarly, following policy congruence theory, the

Danes' and Finns' move to the ECR from the EFD (in which they had sat alongside UKIP and other parties), implies that in 2014 they were a better fit with the ECR than with either the EFD or the prospective radical right populist ENF group that Marine Le Pen and Geert Wilders were attempting to set up.

This section will investigate these questions from the perspective of policy positions on the key radical right populist issues of EU integration and immigration, in addition to general socio-economic and social left–right positions. Given the questions set out above, we focus on the three core ECR parties in 2014—the UK Conservatives, Polish PiS and the Czech ODS—along with our two radical right populist cases: the Danish People's Party and the Finns Party. It is important to note that we are considering these parties' positions in 2014, since we are trying to explain alliance logics at that time. Whether parties subsequently shifted positions (as the UK Conservatives have done on European integration) is irrelevant here.

The first dimension we investigate is European integration. Figure 3.1 shows the results from the CHES expert survey (Bakker et al. 2015). Higher values on the x-axis denote more positive positions towards the EU in general, as well as towards its current and future integration, while higher values on the y-axis indicate that the issue was more salient for the party. Looking at the party positions and saliences, we find that all five parties take clearly negative stances towards European integration, but have not changed their positions much between 2009 and 2014. The new partners for the DF and PS are all located in the space between two and the neutral middle, with the good fit between the five parties underlined by the empty pro-EU side of the dimension in figure 3.1. Given, however, that one of our aims is to understand also why the DF and Finns Party did not choose to sit with their fellow radical right populists, it is worth noting that the equivalent positions on European integration of key ENF parties like the Front National (1.2) and Lega Nord (1.4) would have provided equally good, if not better, matches on this issue. While the positions of the ECR parties on European integration have not changed particularly between 2009 and 2014, the saliences have. As we can see, this increased generally by about four scale points. Importantly, Figure 3.1 indicates that the change in salience was a common move for all parties and one that neither brought them closer together nor pushed them further apart.

This general lack of convergence regarding European integration between 2009 and 2014 is confirmed by the standard deviations between the positions and saliences of the parties. The standard deviation is a simple measure of dispersion, whereby larger values denote more disagreement between the parties. If the theory of policy congruence holds, we should see group formation at times of least disagreement. However, the standard

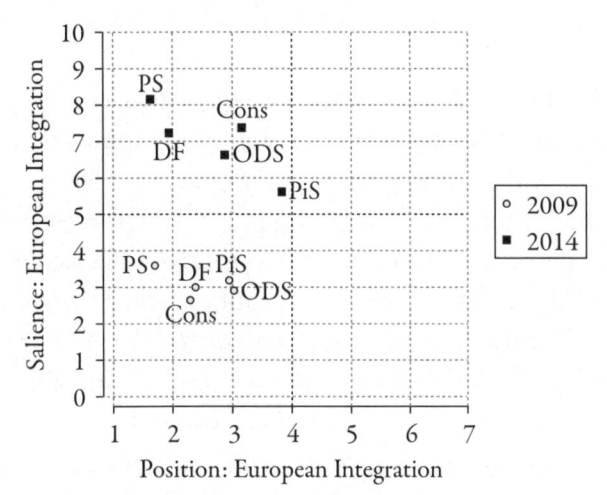

Figure 3.1: ECR parties in 2009 and 2014, European integration

*[Scatter plot showing Salience: European Integration (y-axis, 0–10) versus Position: European Integration (x-axis, 1–7). 2014 points (filled squares): PS (~1.7, 8.2), Cons (~3, 7.4), DF (~2, 7.3), ODS (~3, 7), PiS (~3.8, 5.6). 2009 points (open circles): PS (~1.7, 3.5), DF (~2.5, 3.2), PiS (~3, 3.3), ODS (~3.2, 3), Cons (~2.5, 2.7).]*

Source: Own calculations based on Chapel Hill Expert Survey data (Bakker et al. 2015).

deviations for EU position and salience in 2009 were 0.6 and 0.4, respectively, and slightly increased to 0.9 and 1.0 in 2014. Furthermore, in 2014, the level of disagreement was higher than between all radical right populist parties, which had a standard deviation of only 0.5. In other words, the Danish DF and the Finnish PS joined the ECR at a time when they disagreed more with the three core ECR parties on European integration, even though disagreement was still generally low. For the Danes and the Finns, the ECR is also a worse fit regarding EU integration than the EFD was when they joined it in 2009. The standard deviations in the 2009 EFD were 0.7 for the EU position and 0.6 for EU salience. Both of these values are lower, and thus a better fit, than the ECR in 2014.

A different picture appears when we focus on the second central dimension for radical right populist parties, which is their positions on immigration. Here, larger values denote more negative and, thus stronger, anti-immigration positions as well as greater salience. Since immigration is one of the key policy issues for radical right parties, it is reasonable to assume that it features high on their list of priorities when choosing alliance partners. Nonetheless, Table 3.2 shows that the DF and PS are further away from the ODS, Conservatives and PiS than on European integration. While the five parties all prefer more restrictive immigration policies to some extent, we can identify two relatively clear groups with a gap of nearly two scale points. ODS, PiS and the UK Conservatives are grouped around a value of 7 and their positions did not change particularly between 2009 and 2014. In contrast, the two Nordic radical right populist parties took positions of a value around 9. This is again much closer to the parties both in the ENF (e.g., Front National 9.8, Vlaams Belang 9.6) and in the EFDD (UKIP 9.4, Sweden Democrats 9.8). In short, DF and PS do not fit well on immigration with ODS, PiS and the Conservatives, but rather are close on this issue to all other radical right populist parties (the standard deviation of a hypothetical combined group was 0.5).

Table 3.2: Positions on immigration and deviation within ECR

| Year | UK Cons | DF | PS | ODS | PiS | Deviation |
|------|---------|-----|-----|-----|-----|-----------|
| 2014 | 6.8 | 9.1 | 9.1 | 7.3 | 7.1 | 1.1 |
| 2009 | 6.6 | 9.4 | 8.8 | 7.1 | 7.4 | 1.2 |

Source: Own calculations based on Chapel Hill Expert Survey data (Bakker et al. 2015).

The data for the salience of immigration is less easy to compare. This is because we have a direct expert judgement of immigration salience in 2009, but only have judgements regarding immigration being one of the 'most important issues' (or not) for the parties in 2014. In 2009, we find a wide variation among the saliences of immigration between the five parties. While this issue was judged to be of very limited importance for PiS and ODS (with values around 3 and 4 on a 0 to 10 scale) and of relatively low importance for the UK Conservatives (with a value of 6), it was deemed of utmost importance for the Danes and the Finns (9.3 and 8.4, respectively) who allied with the EFD that year. Thus, in 2009 we indeed saw a divide. In 2014, the picture had changed, albeit not in a way that helps to explain the ECR group formation. Immigration was judged to be the most important issue for the Danes and the second most important issue for both the UK Conservatives and the Polish PiS. On the other hand, immigration did not feature among the three most important issues listed by the CHES experts for the Finns, nor for the Czech ODS. Thus, while some of the parties had indeed converged, a new divide had opened up.

Figure 3.2 sums up the positions of the five parties on the economic and the social left–right dimensions, which run from 0 (left) to 10 (right). On both dimensions, all five parties' positions are unchanged between 2009 and 2014 and we find two very distinct clusters. The UK Conservatives and the Czech ODS take right-

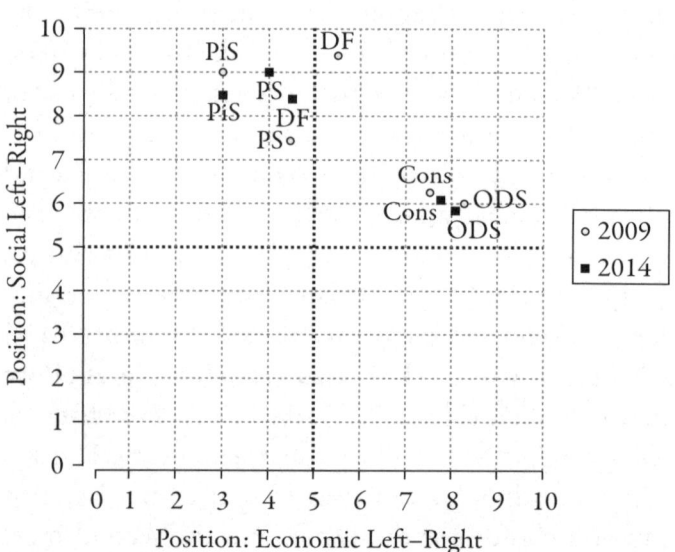

Figure 3.2: ECR parties 2009 and 2014, left–right positions

Source: Own calculations based on Chapel Hill Expert Survey data (Bakker et al. 2015).

wing positions on both dimensions. However, the Danish People's Party and the Finns Party, as well as the Polish PiS, adopt more conservative positions on the social left–right dimension than the Conservatives and ODS, but centrist or even leftist positions on the economic dimension. The result on the social dimension is consistent with radical right parties often being very socially conservative and thus, matching the social profile of the strongly Catholic PiS. Equally, the result on the economic dimension is in line with the general trend of radical right populists trying to protect the welfare state from both neo-liberal reduction attempts and immigration pressure from globalisation. This puts them in strong opposition to the Conservatives and the ODS, which both profess *laissez-faire* economic policy and the reduction of state spending.

Further investigating how well the group fits together, the standard deviations within the ECR for the two types of left–right positions confirm the interpretation from Figure 3.2. Both standard deviations are clearly larger than for EU integration and immigration and neither changed from 2009 to 2014, being 2.2 and 2.3 on the economic left–right dimension and 1.5 in both years on the social left–right dimension. Thus, there is no convergence that would indicate a better policy fit between these parties in 2014, when the group was formed in this composition, compared to 2009, when the ECR rejected the Danes and the Finns. For the two

Nordic parties, the switch from EFD to ECR also did not result in a better matching group. On the contrary, the standard deviations in the EFD were more than half a scale point smaller than in the ECR (1.8 on the economic and 0.9 on the social left–right dimension). This confirms again that the policy congruence for the DF and PS in 2014 would have been higher with the other radical right populist parties, especially as their economic left–right positions had a standard deviation of only 0.5.

To summarise, the results so far indicate that, while the Danish People's Party and the Finns Party may have a broad positional fit with the three core ECR parties, there is substantial variation. DF and PS in 2014 adopted the hardest Eurosceptic positions, although they did not advocate for their countries' exit from the EU (unlike their former EFD ally, UKIP). Similarly, while all five parties held positions favouring stricter immigration policies, the two radical right populist parties had the most negative views. With regard to the social and economic left–right dimensions, the Danes and the Finns' only close fit was with the Polish Law and Justice Party (PiS), which since 2014 has arguably developed into a radical right party itself (Stanley and Cześnik 2019). At the same time, their leftist positions on the economic dimension put DF and PS at odds with the UK Conservatives and the Czech ODS, which have much more liberal economic positions. Thus, while there does not seem to be strong disagreement between these five parties on any of the policy dimensions, they also do not seem to fit particularly well. Importantly, we do not find an increasing congruence that could explain why the group did not accept the Danish DF and the Finns in 2009 but did include them in 2014. Nor do we find that the ECR in 2014 was a more policy congruent group for the Danes and the Finns than the EFD was. Furthermore, a hypothetical group of radical right populist parties—including the ENF parties, UKIP, SD, DF and PS—would also have been a better fit.

## *ECR office spoils*

The spoils of EP office also cannot explain why the Danish DF and the Finnish PS moved from their position alongside UKIP in the EFD, to the UK Conservative-led ECR. It is true that the ECR was a larger and more stable group than the EFDD. However, it is not clear that the spoils offered by the ECR to the DF and PS were any greater than they would have been had these two parties remained alongside UKIP or joined the other radical right populists in the ENF. Firstly, there is no evidence that the two parties gained financially by being in the ECR. Table 3.3 shows that if the amounts received by the ECR and EFDD groups from the EP in 2017 were allocated to parties based on their numbers of MEPs, there was no significant gain for the PS and DF.

Table 3.3: Financial resources per MEP, EFDD and ECR 2017

| Group | MEPs* | EP Allocation, Euro | Per MEP, Euro |
|---|---|---|---|
| EFDD | 45 | 3,653,679.55 | 81,193 |
| ECR | 74 | 6,199,791.15 | 83,781 |

Notes: This does not take into account European party foundations contributions, donations, assets etc.
* Mid-year number of MEPs.
Sources: EFDD 2018, p. 9; ECR 2018, p. 6.

A further, albeit more indirect, source of funding available to parties is through so-called Europarties and affiliated foundations. These exist purely at the European level; their members are national party organisations and their fundable activities are limited to informational and campaigning events directly linked to the EU level. Although membership of both is not obligatory, the Europarty linked to the ECR is the Alliance of Conservatives and Reformists in Europe (ACRE). Given its size, ACRE's funding was considerable, rising from a maximum of €1,400,000 in 2013 to €1,950,000 in 2015 (Directorate-General for Finance 2018). Since the EFD did not have its own affiliated Europarty, joining the ECR offered an additional financial incentive for the Danes and the Finns by providing access to ACRE and its campaigning resources. However, while the Finns joined ACRE in November 2015 and could thus benefit from this funding, the Danes never formally joined the Europarty.

Furthermore, MEPs from the two Nordic parties did not receive any significantly better positions within the EP by switching from the EFD to the ECR. The only influential position was the group vice-chair, which was held by Morten Messerschmidt (DF) in both groups. All other MEPs of both the DF and the PS in the two parliaments (2009–2014 and 2014–2019) were only committee members.

## *Explaining the ECR: marrying up, not down*

We have shown that the dominant theory to explain EP group formation—positional congruence—and the 'office-driven' logic cannot explain how the ECR took the form it did in 2014. We therefore turn to our interviews and explore three interrelated questions: (1) Why did the ECR accept the DF and PS in 2014 but not in 2009? (2) Why did the DF and PS leave the EFD for the ECR? (3) Why did the DF and PS rule out an alliance with the ENF parties and SD, even though the policy position fit was better, especially on immigration?

## Why did the ECR accept the Danes and Finns?

As we have seen, 2014 was not the first time that the Danish People's Party and the Finns Party had sought to join the ECR. Both parties had wished to do so in 2009, but were turned down and subsequently joined the

UKIP-led EFD group. In this section, we examine why the ECR changed its mind about these two Nordic parties in the five years after 2009, and also why it did not admit the Sweden Democrats (or any other radical right parties beyond the DF and PS) in 2014.

From our interviews, it is clear that the UK Conservatives' delegation was the driving force in deciding which parties could join the ECR, especially before 2014. As the German AfD MEP Hans-Olaf Henkel told us, when discussing a preliminary meeting that his party had about joining the group before the 2014 EP elections, 'it was very obvious the ECR was basically dominated by the Conservatives', although he notes that 'after the elections, the importance of the Poles grew', given their increased size. We can see this predominant role of the Conservatives in the accounts of why the DF and the PS were refused admission in 2009.

According to Messerschmidt (DF), 'we never formally applied' in 2009, but 'there was a dinner ... and we were just told that, at the time, they were not ready [to admit the DF]'. In his view, this was 'a strategically—for them, at least—clever decision to wait, with enlargement of parties that are, in my view, entirely rational and democratic and so on, but which have been accused in the media of not being so'. In other words, he attributed the wariness of the ECR in 2009 to the potential domestic reputational costs of being associated with parties like his own. This reading of events is supported by our interview with van Orden (UK Conservatives), who clarified that the Conservatives in the UK were more risk averse than those in Brussels regarding which parties the ECR should accept. He says:

> Don't forget, this was a sensitive time. We're talking about 2008, 2009, with the prospect of a British general election in 2010. So, naturally, London was highly sensitive to anything that might in any way damage the reputation of the Conservatives in London. So they were hypersensitive on all of these sorts of issues. There were certain parties which to our minds were perfectly acceptable at that time but they, London, was, if you like excessively cautious then, but subsequently, you know ... times are now different.

In particular, it seems that the problem for the Conservatives lay with the Danish People's Party. Dan Hannan, one of the most prominent UK Conservative MEPs of the past decade, and a key figure in eventually bringing the DF and PS into the ECR, explained to us in 2014 how their evaluation process had worked in 2009:

> We went through what the British embassies in Helsinki and Copenhagen were saying about them, we looked at what opponents of theirs were saying in those countries. In the case of the Danes we decided they weren't quite ready ... because they had a recent dodgy past, there had been statements from some of their members, which they had been too slow to distance themselves from.

Hannan singles out the former DF MEP (1999–2009), Mogens Camre, who had made controversial statements about Muslims, including a comparison of them to Nazis, and had also claimed that Bulgarians and Romanians were less intelligent than Danes, Finns and Swedes.[4] Hannan told us: 'we definitely felt his views were not compatible with ours. He was obsessed with immigration, obsessed with Islamisation'. He added that 'the test is, how does the party leadership deal with it when that happens?' The DF had apparently been too slow to distance themselves. The leading DF MEP Messerschmidt was also a source of concern, having been convicted in 2002 for offences involving racism. As we will see throughout this book, fear of the domestic costs of being associated with certain parties at the European level is a key explanatory factor for why RRPs finish up in the groups they do.[5]

In contrast, the Finns Party seem to have been much less of a reputational concern to the Conservatives in 2009. Hannan says, 'In the case of the Finns, to be honest we just missed a trick there. By the time we had satisfied ourselves that they were okay in 2009, they had already made a decision to go somewhere else'—that place was, of course, to the EFD with the Danes. The Finns Party MEP and leader at the time, Timo Soini, apparently told Hannan, 'Look, I've now shaken hands with Farage and I've told him it's for five years, so you're too late'. Hannan adds, however, that Soini 'was very clear that it was only for five years and he was very clear with Farage about that'. As we will see in the next chapter, UKIP interviewees have a different view of how clear the Finns were. Our interview in 2017 with the leading Polish Law and Justice (PIS) MEP, Ryszard Czarnecki, confirmed that it was the Conservatives who determined the 2009 exclusion of the two Nordic parties. He explained that his party was 'more open for co-operation' with the Danes and Finns in 2009, but respected the argument of the Conservatives ('our most important partner') that it would be 'very controversial' in the British media and therefore unwise in the year before a general election.

Given that the Conservatives were once more in the year prior to a UK general election when the 2014 EP elections occurred, what made them change their minds about accepting the Danish People's Party? Several factors emerged from our interviews. First, the veto on the DF was removed because they were less worried about guilt by association and due to the increased salience of immigration. Van Orden explains that:

> I think once you're in office in London, some of the sensitivities are slightly less if you like. I think people acquired a more realistic view of where some of these parties stood. I mean, after all, the thing about the Danish People's Party was that they were very strong on the immigration issue. Well it just happened, if you go back to 2009, this was not something the Conservative

Party wanted to talk about. Well you know, times have moved on and immigration after all has gone up very high now on the list.

The DF's image at both European and national levels had also improved in the eyes of the Conservatives. Messerschmidt had not caused controversy while in the EFD since 2009 and had been the main member of that group to become involved in the work of the parliament (something that distinguished Eurosceptic Conservatives from those in UKIP, as we will see later). Moreover, the DF at national level had not only chosen a staider leader in 2012, but had also seen its vote rise to record levels at the 2014 EP elections and appeared closer than ever to taking seats in cabinet. Hannan therefore told us in 2014:

> The Danish People's Party, since the last election, has acquired a new leader, Kristian Thulesen Dahl. He has come without any of the baggage that went with the previous regime. He is spoken of as a future minister, even a future prime minister. So there's been a real shift there, it's seen as a potential party of government.

Meanwhile, the channel of communication between the Conservatives in the EP and the two Nordic parties had remained open. Van Orden says he 'made a point of maintaining good relations with them' and had explained to them that it was more a case of 'not now' than 'never'. For their parts, both the DF and PS were keen to try again with the ECR. Hannan told us that 'the Finns and Danes had been signalling to us literally for years that they were planning to move at the end of the parliament'. According to him, 'they were unhappy with the EFD, it wasn't participating in the work of the parliament, they weren't getting anything done, the whole approach they found incompatible with what they'd come for'. Indeed, Messerschmidt says that they were even 'open for the idea if there suddenly should be a chance to do it in the seventh legislature [i.e. 2009–14], but it never really materialised in a way that could be done'.

Another factor that made the Conservatives more amenable to accepting the Danes in 2014 was that they could not have got the Finns Party without them, since the two Nordic parties presented themselves as a package deal, together with Bas Belders, the Dutch MEP from the EFD. Messerschmidt, who was appointed as negotiator for the three aspirant parties, explained that 'the Dutch, the Finns and us—we had committed ourselves that if we go, we go together'. He adds that this 'gave us more strength because not only could we present and propose three delegations, which of course was important for the constitution of the groups as well, but also seven MEPs, all representing relatively small countries'. For the ECR, which did not have any members from Denmark or Finland, this was a further incentive given that their primary objective in 2014 was, according to van Orden, to 'widen as much as possible our reach. So, we wanted more and more countries'.

An additional incentive for the Conservatives was the effect that taking three country delegations from the EFD might have on UKIP. As van Orden acknowledged:

> A secondary consideration of course was indeed undermining the ability of UKIP to form a political group, particularly prior to a British general election when UKIP after all was sort of running its main operations in the UK, based on the platform they had and the resources they had from the European Parliament.

Hannan presents a different view, arguing that 'if our aim had been to collapse them, then we would have taken the Lithuanians' (referring to the MEP Rolandas Paksas in the EFD). However, we know from our interviews that Law and Justice were not willing to accept Paksas, due to his controversial past and alleged Russian links. It is true though, as Hannan also points out, that the ECR could have taken the Sweden Democrats, who wished to join in 2014, but were turned down and eventually accepted by the EFDD (thus allowing UKIP to form a group). When asked to explain why they had made this distinction between the Nordic populists, Hannan replied that it was due to their very different histories. This, as we shall see in this and succeeding chapters, is key in evaluations by parties of potential RRP partners:

The Danish People's Party began as a popular anti-tax movement and then broadened into Euroscepticism and strict immigration. The Finns Party began as a rural party and then had this gap in the market, because all the others had compromised themselves by backing the Euro and this was their opportunity. The Sweden Democrats were a different thing, they really were a racist party, so a different thing.

Why did the Danes and Finns leave EFD for ECR?

As we have seen, the Conservative Party felt able in 2014 to take the risk of bringing in two radical right populist parties, the Danish DF and the Finnish PS. However, this leaves a question: why did the Danes and Finns choose to move from the EFD, where they had sat alongside parties with whom they enjoyed better policy congruence? One reason cited by interviewees was the different approach of the ECR to its role in the EP, compared to the EFD. In short, the ECR was considered a better resourced and organised group that genuinely engaged with parliamentary work, something that was important for the DF and PS since they wished to be taken seriously domestically as plausible parties of government. As the Finns Party MEP (and leader since 2017) Jussi Halla-aho told us in 2015, 'It was clear that the EFD is not a very well-organised group, which is very important for a small national delegation because we don't have all the officials that we need'. Karsten Lorentzen (DF Foreign Policy advisor and senior EP official for the party from 2009–14) explained their dissatisfaction with this aspect of the EFD in more depth:

> The EFD group was, you could say, not taking the issues very seriously. I remember the group meetings. I mean, they had serious discussions in the other groups, but our group meetings, if they lasted half an hour, it was a long meeting because everything, legislation was dealt with in a very, very superficial manner. Because the Brits [UKIP], they voted "no" to everything. I mean, they didn't even read the amendments or anything. They just voted "no" and that was not satisfying for us because we actually wanted to stay in the EU.

Lorentzen's last point, that the DF (unlike UKIP), wanted to stay in the EU, was raised by other DF and PS interviewees. Despite the Chapel Hill positions on European integration showing the DF and PS as closer on this issue to pro-exit parties like UKIP and the PVV (see Chapters 4 and 5), in fact both the DF and PS were, in 2014, arguing for major reform of the EU, to be achieved by working within its institutions rather than rejecting it. When asked in 2014 about the main driver of the decision to leave EFD for the ECR, the Finns Party MEP Sampo Terho said: 'UKIP is so determined on the exit. They simply want out and they say it out loud, and that's pretty much all they say in the parliament'. He added that 'even though we very much sympathise with them, and some day we could be an exit party, at the moment we are not'.

Beyond positions on Europe and the approach to EP work, what comes through strongly in our interviews is that both the DF and the PS believed significant national-level image-related benefits could be acquired from sitting alongside the UK Conservatives in the EP. Halla-aho told us clearly in 2017 that 'it was to a large extent an image thing for us to leave the EFDD and join the ECR, mainly because of the British Conservatives'. Indeed, he asserted in our 2015 interview that, because of these likely benefits, 'our domestic rivals campaigned very hard against our joining the ECR, because they understood what that would do to our image'. In other words, the PS joining the ECR would show, as Halla-aho put it, 'that we are a respectable party. We are taken seriously in Europe and not everybody else is as hysterical towards us as our rivals in Finland'.[6] Thus, ECR membership provided the PS with a mechanism by which to obtain a 'reputational shield' (Iversflaten 2006) against attacks for being an extreme or trivial party.

The DF interviewees expressed similar views about the domestic image benefits of partnering the UK Conservatives in Europe, especially compared to sitting alongside UKIP and the other EFD parties. The Danish People's Party MEP, Anders Vistisen, explained to us in 2014 that, 'you can say the EFD didn't give us anything in the Danish public perception. They didn't hurt us but they didn't give anything'. In contrast, being with the Conservatives, an internationally well-known mainstream party which had been in power in the UK since 2010, was considered something that 'can aid us instead of just being a neutral thing for us'. Messerschmidt elaborated:

> It gives a lot of credibility. You have your photo taken with the prime minister of the UK and all this. It makes it impossible to say that you're just a populistic, unserious, temporary movement. It makes it clear that in a European context, we are a party which is expected to be—that can be—in government.

Thus, our interviews indicate that the respectability conferred by ECR membership—and in particular by the UK Conservatives—marked the achievement of a long-term goal for the Danish People's Party and the Finns Party. At national level, they were parties that could either sit in government (Finland) or prop up governments in exchange for policy concessions (Denmark).[7] And at European level, they could be accepted as partners by respectable parties of government like the UK Conservatives. Being part of the ECR thus represented a milestone in their journey towards respectability.

Why did the Danes and Finns not ally with ENF?

As we have discussed above, for the DF and the PS, the European-level company they were seen to keep in 2014 was important. But so too was the company they were seen not to keep. If the Conservatives were regarded as positive in terms of domestic image benefits, and UKIP as neutral, other radical right populists like the Front National and the Austrian Freedom Party were seen as decisively negative. As Vistisen said to us in 2014 when asked about the DF's relations with other RRP parties, 'Most of the parties who want to be affiliated with us would primarily give us problems or not do anything for us at all'.

These problems can be broadly categorised as those stemming from present behaviours and those caused by 'toxic' histories. As regards the first, some of the other radical right populist parties were seen as being too unpredictable and risky by the DF and PS, since they contained people prone to making controversial statements that would then be seized upon by Danish and Finnish domestic media and mainstream politicians. As Halla-aho explained to us in 2015:

> Once you formally affiliate to something or associate with somebody, you become guilty by association if the other party does something or says something. So you have to ask yourself the question: what are the benefits for taking this risk of associating with somebody for whose actions you cannot directly affect, but for whose actions you will ultimately take part of the responsibility?

The second problem is one of history: parties like the Front National, Austrian Freedom Party, Sweden Democrats and Vlaams Belang all have extreme right histories and associations with fascism that can make them undesirable for parties seeking domestic mainstream respectability, like the DF and PS. For example, while interviewees acknowledged that the FN under Marine Le Pen had made positive changes, they still felt that the memory of Jean-Marie Le Pen and the continuing negative international image of the party made it unacceptable as an EP partner. As Messerschmidt said, 'It is unthinkable that we would sit in the same group' as FN, although the reason was 'more the heritage after the father and of course the history of the party'. Halla-aho in 2015 made similar points, adding that the FN's style of politics and closeness to Putin also created a problem for his party, especially given Finland's history with Russia. This relationship with Putin and their perceived 'pro-Russian' positions was also, incidentally, the key reason cited by Czarnecki of Law and Justice as to why his party would be reluctant to sit in the same group as the FN or FPÖ.

Like the FN, the FPÖ were also said to have a problem with overcoming their history. Messerschmidt observed to us that 'there is a clear association with Nazism and they have not at all been willing to distance themselves from that past, through the years'. Vistisen similarly pointed to their extremist roots and allegations of their anti-Semitism, explaining that the reasons why the DF could not ally with them were 'very much about history', because:

Some of these parties have had a history that, from our perspective, you cannot come back from. One of them is that party. You can say we don't prioritise to have a larger group [of right-wing Eurosceptics] if we would have negative—really negative—press in Denmark.[8]

Another party with an extreme right past, the Sweden Democrats, was seen as too toxic for admission to the ECR in 2014 not only by the Conservatives (as Dan Hannan's earlier quote explained), but also by the DF. Vistisen told us in June 2014 that 'we really have a hard time with them, both because of their history, where they came from. They've changed a lot, but it's hard for us to overlook that'. Similarly, Lorentzen observed, 'They have changed a lot ... but it's also again, it's their past. I mean, they were neo-Nazis. They came, they had their roots—political roots—in the neo-Nazi scene'.

Interestingly, just as the DF had been seen by the UK Conservatives in 2009 as too slow to clamp down on racism within their party, the SD were similarly judged in 2014 by the DF. Vistisen explained to us:

We have always said if anyone ... had racist views, we will kick them out. It would not be like a month, it would be in the next hour. If someone expressed other unacceptable views from our point of view, they would be kicked out. There is no tolerance for being intolerant in the Danish People's Party. The Swedish Democrats didn't have that line and therefore ... we do not want to be affiliated with them too strongly, simply because we think that they cannot have their own house in order. So they are a loose cannon, in that sense.

While the SD's past image and some of its present actions were considered obstacles to co-operation, its policies were not mentioned by any interviewee as posing a problem. Indeed, in our 2015 interview, Halla-aho told us: 'There are people in our party who won't admit it and who wouldn't like this to be said, but I think in most questions, we are also very close to the Sweden Democrats, who have a very bad reputation'.[9] Returning to the point about domestic reputational costs trumping policy congruence, he added: 'The facts are not the only important thing, it's also important how things appear'. Nonetheless, when asked whether he could see the SD being an acceptable ally for the DF and PS in the post-2019 parliament, he replied, 'Yes, I would hope so very much'.

Interviewees cited similar 'historical baggage' reasons for why the Vlaams Belang would also be a problematic partner, but the same did not apply to Wilders' Party for Freedom. As Messerschmidt pointed out: 'Geert Wilders is a bit different, actually, because he has a past in the ALDE group. Basically, he's a liberal that just saw the problem with Islam and then, of course, made that his almost sole agenda'. While Wilders therefore does not have the same toxic, extreme right aura as the FN or FPÖ, his perceived sole focus on the issue of Islam did create some disquiet.[10] Messerschmidt explained that

'Either you agree one hundred per cent or then you don't agree, whereas if you have the full program that my party has, it's all fair to say that, "Yeah, there are issues where we agree and there are issues where we don't"'. Halla-aho, in 2017, made a similar point to us about the PVV.

> It seems to me that whatever the subject of the meeting, they always make the same speech about Islamisation and immigration and although I substantially agree with them, it makes them sound and look a bit silly when it seems that they aren't even listening to what other people are talking about.

There are strong reasons, therefore, underlying the 2014 decisions of the Danish DF and Finnish PS not to ally with other radical right populist parties. Mostly, as interviewees acknowledged, these concerned fears about image at the national level, especially in relation to the media. Indeed, as Lorentzen of the DF says, 'We let the media decide who we're going to let in and not and I think that's a bit of a problem. The media, they're in charge somehow'. Similarly, the PS's Terho observes that what 'makes it a bit more difficult to join all the forces is that in our own respective countries the press is always making devils out of the new parties of the other countries'. Parties like the DF and PS, which both had national elections approaching in the year after the 2014 EP took office, thus feared the effects of being tainted by association with many other radical right parties, but also chased the benefits of respectability by sitting alongside mainstream ones.

## *The respectable marriage theory*

We can explain the behaviour of the Danish People's Party and the Finns Party through our 'respectable marriage' theory. While scholars have identified policy congruence as the main driver of party group formation in the EP, we have shown how the Danish People's Party and the Finns Party defied this theoretical mechanism in 2014. Building on Ivarsflaten's idea of radical parties needing a 'reputational shield' (2006) and our findings above, we therefore suggest an alternative theory of party group formation: that of the respectable marriage.

This mechanism ranks the party goal of domestic 'votes' and, potentially, 'national office' before EP-group policy congruence and rests on the belief of some party elites that European-level alliances have national-level effects. In other words, parties considered extreme by many voters and which may be un-coalitionable (or at least, not preferred partners) for their country's mainstream parties believe they can use their EP group choices to improve their national situation. The central mechanism of this is to gain respectability in the eyes of national publics and/or prospective coalition partners, by allying in the EP with more moderate parties and not with those foreign parties seen by national publics and elites as more radical. For the Danish DF and Finnish PS in 2014, we have seen how its function was to show, through EP alliances, that they were not like most other RRP parties and could sit comfortably alongside mainstream parties.

It is important to note that this theoretical explanation of EP group formation does not assume that the mechanism of respectability then works domestically. Whether national voters and mainstream parties really pay attention to, or care about, the alliances of radical parties in the EP is not the point. Since our theory is only intended to explain party behaviour in the EP, it is sufficient that the party itself believes in these potential respectability gains. Our theory can also provide insights into subsequent group formation behaviour. Once a party has made the step away from a radical, but policy congruent, group to a less congruent, but more respectable, set of partners, it seems unlikely that it will move back and risk losing the 'respectability bonus' unless the images in their countries of many foreign RRP parties change very significantly.

*Conclusion*

In this chapter, we have shown that in 2014 the ECR was a group made up of two sub-groups. On the one hand, the original members from UK Conservatives, the Polish PiS and the Czech ODS formed the Eurosceptic but mainstream right core of the group. On the other hand, they were joined by two radical right populist parties, the Danish People's Party and the Finns Party. Analysing their policy positions using Chapel Hill Expert Survey data, we find that these parties fit relatively well with regards to their Euroscepticism, but formed two very clear camps in terms of immigration as well as social and economic policies. Moreover, when we looked at the Danes' and Finns' Eurosceptic positions, we found that—like their immigration, social and economic policies—they fitted much better with those of other radical right populist parties in the EFDD and ENF. This raised a number of questions about, firstly, why the ECR would accept ill-fitting radical right parties in 2014 that they had rejected for fear of being tainted by association in 2009 and, secondly, why the Danes and the Finns joined this group rather than the more ideologically compatible EFDD or ENF. We investigated these questions through our interviews with key figures from the ECR member parties.

The entrance of the Danes and the Finns into the ECR was made possible by the desire of the existing ECR parties to form a larger group, by the possibilities it offered to damage UKIP's chances of forming its own group and, importantly, by a lack of fear on the part of the UK Conservatives—the dominant party in the group—that they could be domestically damaged by international co-operation with the Danish People's

Party and the Finns Party. Domestic considerations were also central to the motivations of the Danes and the Finns to join the ECR. They ruled out any notion of joining the ENF given the reputations and historical baggage of the French Front National and the Austrian Freedom Party. They also judged that a continued association with UKIP, while not damaging, would not have been particularly helpful at the national level. In contrast, the ECR offered perceived benefits in terms of reputation and legitimacy on the national level. Joining that group implied association with well-established, mainstream-right government parties, in particular the UK Conservatives.

Building on this logic, we have proposed a new theory of EP group formation that reflects actions based on the perceived national repercussions and benefits of European-level behaviour. In short, joining mainstream parties in a 'respectable marriage' within the EP can be a goal for radical parties that wish to overcome being considered extreme or un-coalitionable at the national level. As we will see in the next chapter on the EFDD, many elements of this 'respectable marriage' logic are also apparent in the alliances pursued, and not pursued, in 2014 by UKIP and the Sweden Democrats.

4

# EUROPE OF FREEDOM AND DIRECT DEMOCRACY

## AN ACCEPTABLE MARRIAGE OF CONVENIENCE

Europe of Freedom and Direct Democracy (EFDD) is often viewed as a successor group to the similarly-named Europe of Freedom and Democracy (EFD) from the 2009–2014 parliament. However, the groups only have two parties in common: UKIP, the largest and core party of the EFDD, and the small Lithuanian delegation from Partija Tvarka ir Teisingumas (PTT—Order and Justice). In fact, the EFDD was the fourth group for UKIP during its two decades in the European Parliament, after having passed through Europe of Democracies and Diversities (1999–2004), Independence/Democracy (2004–2009), and the EFD (2009–2014). The EFD and the EFDD in particular have been characterised by UKIP's driving role in their creation. The logic underpinning UKIP's group formation and how other parties perceived UKIP are, thus, key to understanding the EFDD. As we will see in this chapter, the EFDD was primarily a series of 'marriages of convenience', contracted in order to acquire the visibility and resources provided by being in a group. This understanding was shared by all of its members. The only conditions UKIP set for prospective partners were that there was some shared criticism of the EU and that alliance with them would not damage UKIP's domestic reputation. Unlike the ECR and the ENF, there was no goal to establish a lasting group of parties with shared values.

UKIP's EP groups have all therefore had single-legislature lifespans and have changed greatly in composition from one group to the next. While this upheaval was not a welcome development for the party in 2014, given the effort required to find new partners, it was no surprise. First of all, several EFD members, such as Laikós Orthódoxos Synagermós (LAOS—Greek Popular Orthodox Rally), failed to have MEPs re-elected in 2014. Second, a number of those EFD parties that were returned to the EP were intent on moving to other groups. The Lega Nord (LN—Northern League) under new leader Matteo Salvini had already indicated that its goal after the 2014 elections was to join Marine Le Pen and Geert Wilders in a new radical right populist EP group. In addition, as we saw in the previous chapter, the Dansk Folkeparti (DF—Danish People's Party) and the Finnish Perussuomalaiset (PS—Finns Party) intended to join the ECR in order to improve their domestic reputations. Since the Danes and Finns were negotiating a package deal that included the EFD's Netherlands MEP Bas Belders, this meant the EFD would lose three national delegations to the ECR. As a senior UKIP official, to whom we spoke three times during the 2014–2019 parliament, told us in 2014, they could see how 'EFD could be caught in a pincer movement between an enlarging ECR and Marine Le Pen'.

Nonetheless, when the new EP met in July 2014, once again it was Nigel Farage who was leading a group, not Marine Le Pen. The new EFDD saw UKIP remain as the leading party of its EP group, alongside two parties in parliament for the first time: the populist (but not radical right) Movimento Cinque Stelle (M5S—Five Star Movement) from Italy and the radical right populist Sverigedemokraterna (SD—Sweden Democrats). Their participation, in addition to that of Order and Justice and a collection of individual MEPs, enabled the EFDD to form. At the time of its creation, the EFDD was the smallest group in parliament, with forty-eight MEPs from seven member states at the opening session in July 2014 (see Table 4.1 below). The bulk of its MEPs came from UKIP and M5S (forty-one out of forty-eight) and the group only just met the seven-country requirement. This meant that its continued existence was precarious, since it depended on all parties—and the three individual MEPs from France, Latvia and the Czech Republic—

remaining on board, at least until such time as the group could add more national delegations (see Chapter 6).

Table 4.1: Main members of EFDD

| Party | Country | Vote in 2014 | MEPs in 2014 | Previous EP group |
|-------|---------|--------------|--------------|-------------------|
| UKIP  | UK      | 27.5         | 24           | EFD               |
| M5S   | Italy   | 21.2         | 17           | –                 |
| SD    | Sweden  | 9.7          | 2            | –                 |
| PTT   | Lithuania | 14.3       | 2            | EFD               |

Note: Votes in percentages. Number of MEPs at first session of the new EP in 2014. We only include parties with at least two MEPs. The EFDD also contained three individual MEPs, bringing their overall number to forty-eight.
Source: http://www.europarl.europa.eu/elections2014-results/en/election-results-2014.html

The EFDD's creation and composition raise a number of questions about the alliance logics of its two radical right populist members—UKIP and the Sweden Democrats—which we will answer in this chapter. Those questions are: (1) Given the implosion of the EFD, why did UKIP not simply join with the five radical right populist parties that were trying to form the ENF? After all, they would surely have had considerable policy congruence with them and the group would have been significantly larger than the EFDD; (2) Why were UKIP happy to join forces with M5S, given their apparently considerable policy differences? (3) Since, as we shall see, the reason for avoiding the ENF was the toxic image of parties like the French Front National (FN—National Front), why were UKIP nonetheless willing to accept the Sweden Democrats, a party which also had a lot of toxic historical baggage? (4) Why did the Sweden Democrats not join the ENF parties, with whom—even more than UKIP—they enjoyed strong policy congruence?

We investigate these questions in the same manner as in the previous chapter: through Chapel Hill Expert Survey results, office spoils data and interviews with eight key figures from EFDD parties, some of whom we interviewed on more than one occasion between June 2014 and October 2018. Interviewees included current and former MEPs, in addition to senior national-level MPs and key party officials who could shed light on the logics and processes behind their EP alliances.[1] As the chapter will show, we find that, unlike the Danish People's Party and the Finns Party, UKIP was less concerned with the domestic benefits of EP alliances. However, like those two parties, it was very alert to the potential domestic costs of such alliances. Overall, UKIP's main aim, once it was satisfied that an alliance with a specific foreign RRP party would not damage its reputation at home, was to construct what UKIP interviewees themselves called 'a marriage of convenience' in order to secure EP group spoils such as financial/administrative resources and the visibility offered by extra speaking time, especially for Nigel Farage. As for the Sweden Democrats, they conformed more to the 'respectable marriage' model pursued by the Danish DF and Finnish PS, seeing European alliances as a vehicle to distance themselves from their domestic pariah status. The end goal of this, they openly acknowledged, was to eventually sit alongside the DF and PS in the ECR; an ambition they achieved in July 2018. Therefore, in the conclusion to this chapter we argue that, over the past decade, UKIP's group—whether the EFD in 2009–2014 or the EFDD—can be seen as a type of 'half-way house' for some radical right populists on their way towards respectable European mainstream shores.

## *The EFDD: an ideologically heterogenous group*

In this section, we consider whether the main explanation given in the political science literature on EP group formation, namely policy congruence, can help to explain the creation of the EFDD and the strategies of its two radical right populist parties, UKIP and the Sweden Democrats. In other words, how well did UKIP, the Sweden Democrats and the Five Star Movement fit together in 2014? Would UKIP and Sweden Democrats have found a more ideologically homogenous home with their fellow radical right populist parties in the ENF group? To answer these questions, we again use Chapel Hill expert data (Bakker et al. 2015) to investigate the fit of these parties in terms of policy positions. Echoing the approach in Chapter 3, we analyse the congruence of the main EFDD parties (UKIP, SD and M5S) on European integration, immigration and the two left–right dimensions. We also examine whether there are obvious policy position differences that might have prevented UKIP and the Sweden Democrats from joining the ENF parties instead.

Figure 4.1 shows the positions on European integration of UKIP, M5S and SD and illustrates their proximity to one another on this issue. Since we want to investigate whether there are differences in the Euroscepticism of UKIP and SD compared to the parties of the ENF that might explain why they are not all in the same group, Figure 4.1 therefore also shows the positions and saliences regarding European integration of the five main ENF parties: the French Front National, Austrian Freedom Party, Dutch Freedom Party, Flemish Vlaams Belang and Italian Lega Nord.

For UKIP, SD and the M5S in 2014, we can see a very good match on Eurosceptic positions, although there is a gap between the salience scores of this issue for UKIP and M5S compared to the SD. We also find a good positional fit if we consider UKIP and SD alongside the parties of the ENF. The French FN, Italian LN, and Dutch PVV are all considered to share the same strong Eurosceptic positions of UKIP and SD. Moreover, these three ENF parties also ascribe similar degrees of impor-

Figure 4.1: EFDD and ENF parties 2014, European integration

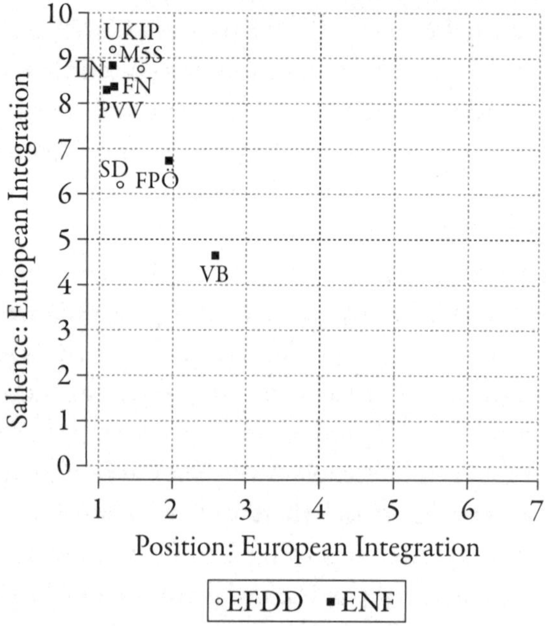
10
9
8
7
6
5
4
3
2
1
0
UKIP
M5S
LN
FN
PVV
SD
FPÖ
VB
Salience: European Integration
1
2
3
4
5
6
7
Position: European Integration
EFDD
ENF

Source: Own calculations based on Chapel Hill Expert Survey data (Bakker et al. 2015).

tance to the topic as UKIP. The Austrian FPÖ is closer to the Sweden Democrats, while Vlaams Belang is the least Eurosceptic of all the ENF and EFDD parties (as noted in Chapter 5, the VB's softer Euroscepticism appears largely due to the EU's importance to the local economy in Flanders). Overall, Figure 4.1 shows how well these parties fit together in the European integration stances, highlighted by the emptiness of the pro-EU side of the dimension.

Investigating the standard deviations of these positions in the EFDD and ENF confirms this finding. The standard deviation, and thus disagreement on European integration is very low among the three EFDD parties (0.5) and slightly higher (0.7) in the ENF as both FPÖ and Vlaams Belang hold less negative positions. While the agreement within the ENF is very high, it would still be so if both UKIP and SD had joined the ENF instead of forming the EFDD (standard deviation of 0.6). The salience of European integration is less congruent but similar in the EFDD and the ENF (standard deviations of 1.7 and 1.8, respectively). Thus, while European integration is not an issue that should have prevented the formation of the group, from a pure congruence perspective the two radical right parties in the EFDD, UKIP and the Sweden Democrats, could just as well have joined the ENF.

The central policy issue for most radical right populist parties is immigration. Table 4.2 summarises the positions that the Chapel Hill experts perceived the EFDD and ENF parties to have held on this issue in 2014. It shows that, in comparison to European integration, the EFDD group has a substantially higher standard deviation and, thus, very low congruence. This is mainly due to the considerably more positive immigration position of the Italian M5S at that time. In contrast, UKIP and the Sweden Democrats agree on strongly anti-immigration positions and were also aligned on this with the ENF parties. Indeed, their agreement is at the same level as that of all radical right populist parties (which was 0.48). In other words, if UKIP and SD had joined the ENF parties, the combined congruence of this hypothetical group on immigration policies would have been even better.

Table 4.2: Positions on immigration and deviation within EFDD

|  | UKIP | SD | M5S | FN | FPÖ | LN | PVV | VB | Deviation |
|---|---|---|---|---|---|---|---|---|---|
| EFDD | 9.4 | 9.8 | 5.3 | – | – | – | – | – | 2.5 |
| ENF | – | – |  | 9.8 | 9.5 | 8.4 | 9.8 | 9.6 | 0.6 |
| UKIP & SD & ENF |  |  | – | – | – | – | – | – | 0.5 |

Source: Own calculations based on Chapel Hill Expert Survey data (Bakker et al. 2015).

As we have explained, the data for the salience of immigration is less easy to compare, since we only have a direct expert judgement of salience for this issue in 2009 (in the 2014 Chapel Hill survey, experts were simply asked to list 'the three most important issues' for parties). Nonetheless, for the EFDD, we see the same divide on salience as we saw for the position on immigration. The Chapel Hill experts judged that immigration was the most important issue for both UKIP and SD as well as all five ENF parties in 2014, while immigration did

EUROPE OF FREEDOM AND DIRECT DEMOCRACY

not feature among the three most important issues for the Italian M5S. This confirms that, for the salience of immigration, UKIP and the Sweden Democrats would, again, have fitted better with their fellow populist radical right parties than with the M5S.

We see a similar picture concerning the parties' positions on the economic and the social left–right dimensions. Figure 4.2 shows that M5S is far away from UKIP and SD on both dimensions, especially the social left–right. Among the seven RRP parties, we see broad agreement on conservative social values which is also

Figure 4.2: EFDD and ENF parties 2014, left–right positions

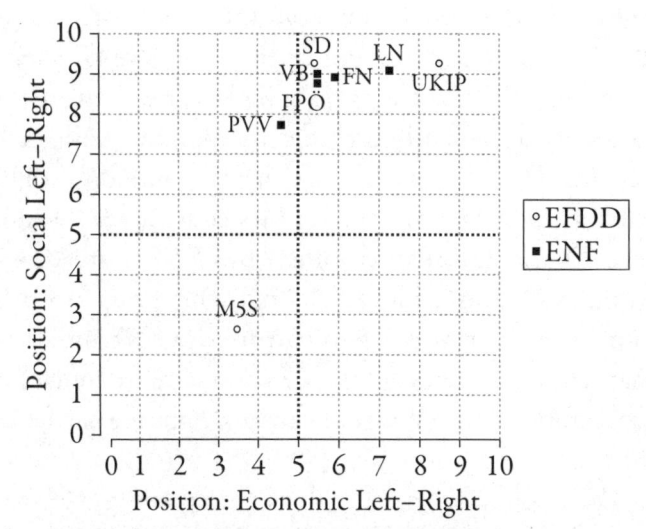

Source: Own calculations based on Chapel Hill Expert Survey data (Bakker et al. 2015).

confirmed by the small standard deviations for the ENF (0.6) and the hypothetical 'ENF plus UKIP and SD' (0.5). The EFDD, however, has a very large standard deviation (3.9) and this incongruence is clearly driven by the much more liberal position at the time of the M5S.

Looking at the economic left–right dimension, we find a larger spread among the RRP parties, with a standard deviation of 2.6 among the EFDD and of 1.0 among the ENF parties. The radical right populist parties' economic positions range from the economically very liberal UKIP to the Dutch PVV (just to the left of the dimension's centre), which is closer to the position of the M5S. This confirms the centrist drift of some radical right populists on socio-economic issues (de Lange 2007), with some moving to more pro-welfare state positions, even if these come in the welfare-chauvinistic variety that explicitly excludes immigrants from such benefits. However, we also see that not all radical right parties have taken this turn (Otjes et al. 2018). Even if the SD and UKIP had joined the ENF instead, we would still find a rather incongruent group on this dimension. That this is also true for the ENF indicates that economic issues do not seem to matter so much for group formation among radical right populist parties in the EP.

Thus, policy congruence does not explain the formation of the EFDD. While UKIP, SD and the M5S had critical stances towards the EU in common, on immigration and the left–right dimensions, we found a sizable disagreement between UKIP and SD on one side and M5S on the other. Moreover, on all four issues and dimensions in our investigation of congruence, both UKIP and the Sweden Democrats would have fit at least as well—and in some cases markedly better—with their fellow radical right populists in the ENF.

## *EFDD office spoils*

To assess the role of office considerations in forming the EFDD, this section looks at financial resources as well as positions within the group and in the EP. The Sweden Democrats, like the Italian Five Star Movement, were not in the parliament before 2014. While SD officially announced, before the 2014 EP elections, that they were open to not joining a group (Bolin 2015: 72), once they had won seats in the EP, they were determined to do so. Likewise, we know from our interviews that UKIP was very anxious to secure the office benefits of greater speaking time and resources. Here, we look briefly at the relative distribution of spoils within the EFDD, to see whether it might have played a role in the decision of parties to be part of this group rather than the ENF.

Table 4.3 shows that the EFDD was able to provide more financial resources per MEP than the ENF. As we discussed in Chapter 2, the allocation of finances to groups depends on both the number of MEPs and the number of country delegations and thus does not scale up one-to-one. Notably, had UKIP's large delegation joined the ENF, this figure per MEP would very likely have been higher.

Table 4.3: Financial resources per MEP, EFDD and ENF 2017

| Group | Year | MEPs* | EP Allocation, Euro | Per MEP, Euro |
|---|---|---|---|---|
| EFDD | 2017 | 45 | 3,653,679.55 | 81,193 |
| ENF | 2017 | 39 | 2,718,648.83 | 69,709 |

Notes: This does not take into account European party foundations contributions, donations, assets etc.
* Mid-year number of MEPs.
Sources: ENF 2018, p. 8; EFDD 2018, p. 9.

As we noted in the previous chapter, in 2014 the ECR offered new entrants the possibility of access to additional funding by joining their linked Europarty, the Alliance of Conservatives and Reformists in Europe. While the EFD had no such organisation, the EFDD founded its own affiliated Europarty in 2014, the Alliance for Direct Democracy in Europe (ADDE), which was recognised by the EU and received its first funding in 2015. In 2015, the maximum funding was set by the EU at €1.25 million and for 2016 at €1.4 million (Directorate-General for Finance 2018). A foundation linked to ADDE, the Initiative for Direct Democracy, also received €730,000 in 2015.[2] While the Sweden

## EUROPE OF FREEDOM AND DIRECT DEMOCRACY

Democrats and some of UKIPs MEPs joined ADDE, the M5S did not. ADDE was disbanded after an audit found that UKIP had broken the rules by spending funds on its 2015 UK general election campaign and the (defunct) Europarty was asked in May 2018 to repay over €1 million.[3]

Apart from the financial resources that can be gained through EP groups, there is a range of positions that can only be accessed by group members. Being in a group is therefore preferable, from an office perspective, to being in the non-inscrits. However, as we have seen in the previous chapter, engaging with the work of the EP was said by Danish People's Party interviewees to have been less important to UKIP in the 2009–2014 EP than it was to them. Investigating the EP positions among the EFDD parties suggests that for the British, this attitude persisted. The only official position a UKIP MEP took up was as the co-chair of the group, and the group's seat in the Conference of Presidents. Similarly, the SD only filled its group-internal leadership seat (the vice-chair). The M5S MEPs, on the other hand, were much more active in taking up these opportunities in the EP. They not only took the EFDD-internal treasurer position, but also that of EP vice-president and two vice-chairs in EP committees.

These findings tally with those of Nathalie Brack (2017b: 401), who shows that the EFD's main activities were in the EP's public arena, in particular giving speeches and asking questions. Indeed, UKIP members are Brack's main examples of the MEP type that is primarily a 'public orator', focusing exclusively on publicising grievances towards the EU in a manner that will generate as much publicity as possible (Brack 2015). Allying with UKIP is thus a double-edged sword for parties interested in influencing the legislative process in the EP. On the one hand, UKIP does not use its numerical strength to demand positions in committees or as rapporteurs, leaving smaller parties to fill them if they wish. On the other, UKIP is not significantly helpful within these processes.

## *Explaining the EFDD: a marriage of convenience*

As we have seen, neither policy congruence nor office seem to be the driving factors behind UKIP's and the Sweden Democrats' decisions to form a group with the Five Star Movement and assorted individual MEPs, rather than with their fellow radical right populists in the ENF. Nor can they help us understand why, if UKIP was concerned about the domestic reputation costs of allying with parties like the Front National, the same logic was not applied to the Sweden Democrats. In the remainder of this chapter, we will therefore consider these questions using the interview material gathered with key figures from the EFDD parties between the period of the group's formation in 2014 and late 2018.

## EUROPE OF FREEDOM AND DIRECT DEMOCRACY

Why did UKIP not join the ENF?

UKIP, in 2014, would have fitted well with ENF parties like the Front National, the Italian Lega Nord and the Dutch PVV on its key policies of opposition to European integration and immigration. Moreover, it would have fitted better with any of the ENF parties on immigration and social/economic left–right issues than it did with its largest EFDD partner, the Five Star Movement. According to the policy congruence theory, UKIP should therefore have jumped at the chance to ally with the group being put together by Marine Le Pen and Geert Wilders. So why did it not do so?

As we saw in the previous chapter, when discussing the Danish People's Party and Finns Party's views of other radical right parties like the Front National, Austrian Freedom Party and Sweden Democrats, UKIP was similarly conscious of potential domestic reputational costs from alliances with controversial parties, especially in the year prior to the 2015 British general election. The senior UKIP official explained to us in 2014: 'It's all to do with perceptions of parties in the UK. It's not just purely history; it's also to do with perceptions'. In particular, UKIP felt that any association with the FN would be damaging, even though—like the DF and PS interviewees—those we spoke to acknowledged that the party had made positive changes under Marine Le Pen. As the UKIP official told us:

> If you say 'Front National' in the UK, the problem is not Marine Le Pen. The problem is not Marine Le Pen's policies. The problem is when you say 'Front National', people immediately think of Jean-Marie Le Pen and all that associated history and his comments over the years ... Just in case there was any doubt, also 'Front National' sounds like 'National Front'. Just if there was any doubt lingering. So the matter is public perception.

The UKIP MEP, Roger Helmer echoed this view of the FN, saying: 'They're moving in the right direction, we ought to reward them for the efforts that they're making, but when all that is said and done, you can just imagine what *The Guardian* would make of it if we sat with the National Front'.

The Austrian Freedom Party was also said to pose a reputational problem for UKIP, due to its extreme right past, and had been refused entry into the EFD in 2011 for that reason, with the Danish People's Party, Finns Party and UKIP opposing and the Lega Nord in favour. Nonetheless, the senior UKIP official we spoke to was more open to the idea of the Austrians being acceptable at some point in the future, commenting: 'As they change and the public perception changes, it becomes easier for ourselves to accept them into the group'.

If the Austrians were a case of 'maybe one day', Wilders' Party for Freedom was one of 'missed your chance'. As we discovered from our interview with Lucas Hartong, the PVV MEP from 2009–2014, his former party was approached by Morten Messerschmidt of the Danish People's Party to join the EFD in 2011. Hartong said that all four PVV MEPs were keen to do so for a number of reasons. First, because they were in the non-inscrits group at the time. Second, as Hartong put it, UKIP 'were Eurosceptic, but they were acceptable for many voters in the Netherlands and Europe-wide'. Third, as Gawain Towler, former spokesperson and press officer for UKIP and EFDD, and Hartong both confirmed, the PVV and UKIP delegations in the 2009–2014 parliament got along very well. Indeed, according to Hartong, while the Front National and Austrian Freedom Party largely 'ignored' the PVV MEPs in those years, 'with Mr. Farage and UKIP there was lots of contact'. Nonetheless, Hartong says that, 'to our astonishment', Wilders would not sanction the move, apparently because he was afraid of having to take responsibility for any controversial actions or outbursts by UKIP and its MEPs. This refusal to join in 2011 allegedly cost Wilders later, since—according to two of our interviewees—the PVV enquired about joining the EFDD after the failure of the ENF to secure enough countries to form a group in 2014. One told us that, although personal relations between the parties in the EP were still good at that point, Farage said 'no'. A possible reason may have been the renewed focus of Wilders on Islam in the 2014 European campaign, with the leader referring to 'Moroccan scum' and seemingly endorsing their being expelled from the Netherlands.[4] As Towler put it to us, 'Nigel doesn't want to bang the Islam drum' and, similar to the UK Conservatives' fears concerning the DF in 2009, UKIP in 2014/15 may have judged association with Wilders, who has a strong international media profile, too potentially costly in domestic terms, in the run-up to the UK general election.

Why did UKIP accept the M5S?

UKIP therefore found itself in a bind after the 2014 EP elections. It had topped the poll in the UK and secured its highest ever number of MEPs, yet it risked being unable to form a group—something that was extremely important to it in terms of visibility and resources, especially in the year before the 2015 UK general election. How could it balance its need to form a group with its need to avoid toxic partners?

One way was to ignore policy congruence on a number of issues and court a party that had secured seventeen MEPs at its first European election: the Italian Five Star Movement. As the Chapel Hill data shows, the two parties were very distant not only on immigration, but also on social and economic left–right issues. And even though the CHES experts place them close to one another on European integration, their positions were in fact quite different on this issue, too. As Roger Helmer observed: 'UKIP's agenda is to get our country out of the European Union. The Five Star Movement doesn't actually want to get Italy out of the European Union'. In fact, while the M5S was very critical of the Euro and European bureaucrats, it wanted to reform the EU and—unlike UKIP—it also wanted to engage fully with the workings of parliament. David Borrelli, the leader of the M5S delegation and co-chair of the EFDD, explained to us in 2014 that the M5S was 'against a European Union based on monetary union which is not reflected in a political and social union', but was in favour of 'a common border, common armed forces, common taxes and common debts'. These views were obviously anathema to UKIP. Moreover, while UKIP agreed to call the group 'Europe of Freedom and Direct Democracy' to reflect the Five Star Movement's calls at the time for greater direct democracy, this was primarily a cosmetic move and not indicative of a deeply-shared policy stance.

Ultimately, the reason why UKIP and M5S were able to sit together, beyond their mutual need to form a group and some shared criticism of the EU, was their strict 'prenuptial' agreement. As Borrelli explains:

> They guaranteed that there would be no type of limitation on how we voted. They also guaranteed that, in any moment and in any commission, we could propose amendments and they would sign them so that we could present them. Then, once in the chamber, each party would vote in line with its own programme and beliefs. We really liked this.

The co-chair of the M5S delegation, Ignazio Corrao, echoed this account in 2015, saying, 'Our condition was that we were given total freedom by the EFDD delegation ... we are not subject to any group discipline, which would have surely created a lot of problems for us'. He added, 'This is a marriage of convenience, but we always said so, it was well known. We never said that we were walking hand in hand with our allies as regards our ideas'. The senior UKIP official made a similar observation in 2014: 'It's a marriage of convenience to get funding and speak to the European Parliament. It's not a political party. It's a group for strategic, pragmatic reasons'. Helmer put it equally bluntly: 'The only reason that we are creating a group together is because there are benefits in terms of administration and staffing and speaking time and all those things. We need to seek those benefits'. In particular, the UKIP official noted, 'The thing is the speaking time—the speaker slot for Nigel is very important', since Farage was able to use it to gain the party a lot of media attention in the UK. Or, as Gawain Towler explained, Farage's main interest in forming a group was 'in order that he could sit in the front row and make his YouTube speeches'. Beyond that, Towler said, Farage 'gets on very well with individuals and he's happy to support them, but he is utterly uninterested in the mechanics of a European parliamentary group'. So much so that Farage was willing to 'trade away staff in order to get people on board' and form a group. Hence, Towler says, 'at no point in any of the groups that we've had, have we had staffing commensurate to our size'. In other words, Farage traded one element of 'office' (staffing) in order to secure another (visibility).

One of the single-member delegations in the EFDD, Petr Mach, from the Strana Svobodných Občanů (SSO—Czech Party of Free Citizens), expressed to us, in 2015, analogous views about the nature and function of the group. Like UKIP, his party advocated its country's exit from the EU. As he explained, therefore, 'It would be better for me and UKIP if there were five more parties similar to us'. However, this was not the case and 'so we had to do some compromises'. Like the Five Star Movement and UKIP interviewees above, he emphasised that the EFDD members were clear about the marriage contract:

> Everyone in our group understands that there are differences and we have no internal obligation to vote together. There are things that connect us like general Euroscepticism, on the other hand any party of our group can use the group as an instrument to propose amendments and so on. If you see an amendment submitted nominally by EFDD group it does not mean that I will vote for it, if it was submitted by Italians. So, we use each other as an instrument.

Why did UKIP accept the Sweden Democrats?

Just as UKIP had to weigh up their lack of policy congruence with the Five Star Movement against their need to form a group, so too they had to balance that latter need against the problematic reputation of the Sweden Democrats. While the SD did not pose any significant policy congruence difficulties for UKIP (with the only noticeable difference being on the economic left–right scale), they did bring reputational risk, given their extreme right history (Rydgren 2008; Bolin 2015). Indeed, in the week after the EP election, Farage publicly said he thought it was 'pretty unlikely' that UKIP would work with SD.[5]

Our interviews suggest that a number of factors contributed to UKIP's eventual admission of the SD, beyond the obvious one that they needed them to make up the numbers. First, SD managed to gain UKIP's trust by their behaviour during the negotiation phase and second, they showed a clear willingness to confront their troublesome past; third, the two SD MEPs were people without controversial pasts and unlikely to cause trouble.

Concerning the first point, we were told that secret negotiations took place between UKIP and the Sweden Democrats while the Five Star Movement was preparing to put its choice of EP partner (i.e. between the EFDD, ECR and the non-aligned group) to an online membership vote (Bressanelli and De Candia 2018).[6] The SD were instructed to keep quiet about these talks since, in UKIP's view, public knowledge of them in Italy might have hindered the chances of M5S members voting to join the EFDD. Despite the intense media interest in what they were going to do in the EP, the Swedes respected this need for silence, thus increasing UKIP's confidence in their reliability.

UKIP also asked the Sweden Democrats to provide a document, setting out their history and their current political philosophies and policies. In particular, they were told to clearly tackle any allegations of racism and xenophobia. We have a copy of the seven-page document they eventually submitted, which is dated 4 June 2014, that is, eight days before the Five Star Movement's vote to join UKIP and well before anything was known publicly about the SD joining. It bears close examination, since it provides unique insights both into how the SD were seeking to position themselves, and why UKIP felt they could accept them.

On the third page, following an explanation that the party the SD considers itself most similar to is the Danish People's Party, there is a section headed 'Is the Sweden Democrats an (sic) "Xenophobic", "Extreme Right" Party?' They note that 'as most other parties in Europe who want to restrict mass immigration, the Sweden Democrats have often been accused by our political opponents and left-wing media for being "extreme", "xenophobic", and "racists"'. In response, they cite several passages from their 'Statement of Principles', which insist the party is democratic, values all human beings and practices a 'version of nationalism' that 'is open and non-racist'. They also note that 'several high-ranking representatives of the Sweden Democrats are of non-Swedish ethnic descent' and draw attention to a 2012 survey showing that 20 per cent of the party's members were of foreign descent.

After this rebuttal regarding the present, in the next section, entitled 'We Acknowledge and Learn from our Mistakes', they state: 'We will not hide the fact that we have made mistakes in our past that have made it a lot easier for our opponents to put these labels on us'. Many of these mistakes were made, they say, between 1991 and 1994 when 'the party was temporarily radicalised due to bad leadership'. In particular, 'the worst of these mistakes was that the party didn't distance itself from radical youths with sub-cultural looks and that these were allowed to participate in some of the party demonstrations'. Since then, they state that 'we have been working very hard to distance ourselves from all forms of extremism, to reform the party, to learn from our mistakes and to change our image'. As part of this, they claim that almost all members from the 1990s have either been expelled or have left and that, when anyone from the SD has expressed xenophobic views, 'in all cases these persons immediately have been expelled from the party'.

We saw in the previous chapter that in 2014, the DF did not seem convinced of the SD's ability to deal with troublesome members, but UKIP appreciated the SD's open acknowledgement of its past. While they would have preferred to take a less controversial party to fulfil the seven-country delegation requirement for forming a group, they were now more willing to consider SD's application. As the UKIP official told us, at this stage UKIP explained to the SD 'that they were not the first port of call, but that we were pleased with the document they gave us, that we were much happier than we were before'. It also helped, as the official explained, that the two SD MEPs elected in 2014—Peter Lundgren and Kristina Winberg—had no history of controversy and seemed unlikely to cause any, since they were 'nice, decent people. Views are run of the mill cultural nationalists. They weren't racist in any way. They personally were not in any way dangerous to us, politically'.

What clinched the Sweden Democrats' entry to the group was both the absence of any better alternative and the fact that the Five Star Movement approved them, having itself joined the group after the online vote). David Borrelli told us that 'we had some doubts about them, because they have an awkward past', but said that 'they gave us strong guarantees', including signing 'a commitment to maintain a certain type of behaviour'. The M5S also appreciated the document about their history that the SD had submitted and discussed at length with them. Borrelli says he concluded therefore that:

> They had a strong desire to 'renew themselves' and to lose a certain label ... joining the EFDD therefore was an opportunity for them and it seemed right for us to grant it to them given the commitment which they wanted to undertake and had signed.

## Why did SD join the EFDD and not the ENF?

Why were the Sweden Democrats prepared to go to great lengths to satisfy UKIP and the M5S that they should be let into the EFDD? After all, they had been courted strongly by the main ENF party, Front National, with whom they not only enjoyed greater policy congruence, but also had a history of good relations stretching back over a decade. While usually vague and evasive regarding his opinions about Front National, SD leader Jimmie Åkesson said in June 2014 that the party had used FN printing presses for their 1998 election campaign brochures and also acknowledged having met Marine Le Pen and had 'a cup of coffee' with her at the Swedish parliament in 2014.[7] Moreover, the SD international secretary, Kent Ekeroth, had been a member of the Europarty, the European Alliance for Freedom (EAF), which included leading politicians from future ENF parties like Front National and the Austrian Freedom Party (see Bolin 2015: 71–72). Yet, much to the disappointment of the ENF parties, the Swedes explored first the possibility of joining ECR—and were swiftly rebuffed—and then eventually managed to join the EFDD's ideologically heterogeneous marriage of convenience. Why?

Again, the answer lies in our 'respectable marriage' theory, set out in the previous chapter. The Sweden Democrats are particularly interesting in this sense, as they are the only radical right populist party in the 2014 EP that on one hand, ruled out alliances with some RRPs (in the ENF) due to their reputations, but on the other, were themselves shunned by other RRPs (in the ECR) for the same reason. They thus ended up the middle ground of UKIP's group, which can be viewed as a sort of European staging post for parties like the DF, PS and SD on the road towards a more mainstream group. From our interviews with them, it is clear that the SD sees itself on a journey from being considered a pariah party, towards becoming one that could be accepted as a partner in power. And, just like the DF and PS, the Swedes saw their alliance choices at European level as crucial in improving their national image and building a 'reputational shield' (Iversflaten 2006). Indeed, these two parties (the Danes in particular) served as models for the SD both domestically and in the EP. As Kent Ekeroth, who was responsible for negotiating their European alliances in 2014, explained to us:

> Both these parties benefit from having been there already for five years. They get normalised, people meet them [and say], "okay they're not Nazis" or whatever they accuse them to be and they're obviously not. We're not, either. So they have that with them and now it's sort of our turn.

As was clear from the document they submitted to UKIP in June 2014, the SD were well aware of the problems that their history and consequent image posed for potential partners. Recalling the comments made by PS and DF interviewees about other parties' images, which we presented in the previous chapter, they too blamed the media (in part) for this. Ekeroth told us that 'we understand if other parties choose not to, or are careful about affiliating themselves with us, not because of who we are but because who they think we are. It's not only media but media can shape perceptions into making others believe something they're not'. Hence, as Richard Jomshof—one of the leading national members of the SD—told us regarding the Danish People's Party's attitude towards the SD in 2014: 'I think that in a way they are afraid of media still, what they might write about us and our background'. On this point, Ekeroth added that, while they had 'good connections' with some in the DF, that party's leading European representative Morten Messerschmidt had deliberately kept his distance from them; this also makes sense given Messerschmidt's own image problems due to past actions.

SD apply the same logic towards their former friends in the Front National and ENF as the Danes did towards them. While Ekeroth acknowledges that he had had 'good relations' with those parties for many years, in 2014 the SD felt they needed to turn their back on them. Echoing what we have already heard from other interviewees about Front National in particular, Ekeroth explains: 'We feel like a lot of these parties have gone in the right direction. For instance, Front

National, Marine is doing good things with it. There are still some problems that we didn't feel 100 per cent comfortable with. So, we rule them out at this stage'.

Once again, a key reason was the anticipated negative reaction from Swedish media, if the SD were to sit with the FN at European level. In particular, the anti-Semitic outbursts by Marine Le Pen's father (who, in June 2014, was still in the party) were considered problematic. When discussing the dangers of proximity to the FN, Ekeroth pointed to 'Jean-Marie Le Pen, who constantly says stuff ... and the Swedish press would love to have that to hold that against us'. Similarly, Jomshof said:

> The main problem with that group at the moment it's not the Austrian party, FPÖ. It's not Vlaams Belang. It's National Front. It's not Marine Le Pen but it's that there are other politicians there. As long as they are part of the party, it's really, really hard for us to be a part of that.

Unlike the DF, PS and UKIP—who also expressed reservations about the Austrian Freedom Party and, to a lesser extent, Vlaams Belang—for the SD in 2014 it seemed to be only the Front National among the ENF parties that posed a significant obstacle. When asked about the Austrian Freedom Party, Jomshof told us in 2014: 'I'm happy for what happens with FPÖ in Austria, for example. I'm really happy for them. I've met them a couple of times and I think that more or less it's a good party'. In our most recent interview with him in

2017, however, Jomshof discussed how Swedish media seemed to differentiate between radical right populists and that this inevitably influences alliance strategies. As he explained:

> Some of the parties in Europe ... I mean, parties like FPÖ, Vlaams Belang, National Front, when you read Swedish media about them, it's not that positive. But the truth is, the Fremskrittspartiet in Norway, the Danish People's Party—they have a different image here in Sweden. Also UKIP actually, and so I think that quite a lot of journalists seem to be quite surprised when we entered the same group as UKIP because I think some of them thought that UKIP would never accept us, but they did. So, of course it was good for our image.

This brings us back to the point earlier about UKIP's group—whether the EFD or the EFDD—being a kind of staging post for some radical right populist parties as they seek to travel towards more respectable shores. Our UKIP interviewees were well aware of this function. As the senior official we spoke to put it, 'It's a bit like a tumble dryer. We take them in, we wash them and then they move somewhere more respectable'. In a similar way, Towler, when discussing the Nordic populist parties, said, 'They're in Europe, in order to use it as a trampoline back into the chancelleries of their own countries'. UKIP was able to assist them with this because, first, since it started off (much like the AfD in Germany) as a party founded by a professor from the London School of Economics, Alan Sked, in the 1990s, it did not have the same historical baggage as parties like the Front National and the Austrian Freedom Party (Usherwood 2016: 248). So, association with UKIP was not going to taint parties domestically in the same way. Second, UKIP had, as we have seen, its own needs and ways of operating in the EP that suited temporary association—it did not impose strict voting discipline and could be treated as a short-term marriage of convenience. The marriage suited both sides. UKIP got to form its group and be with parties that it was confident would not damage it domestically. And radical right populists with national office ambitions like the Danish People's Party, Finns Party and Sweden Democrats had the opportunity to spend a few years improving their image before setting off again towards a more respectable mainstream destination.

*Conclusion*

The two radical right populist parties of the EFDD—UKIP and the Sweden Democrats—were united in 2014 by their simultaneous needs to be in a group and not to be with the parties of the ENF. In order to achieve this, they accepted a marriage of convenience with a party which, although populist, was not manifestly radical right and which did not share most of their main policy positions: the Italian Five Star Movement. As we have seen, while these parties had shared 'office' needs, the motivations of all three differed: UKIP needed the resources and visibility provided by having its own group, but wanted to avoid the bad publicity of association with the likes of the Front National. Beyond that, the party did not see great benefits in its alliance. The Five Star Movement wanted to have the platform and resources provided by the group, but with no restrictions on how it voted in parliament. Finally, the SD saw the EFDD as a stepping stone on the road to respectability. The EFDD marriage of convenience thus gave all three what they wanted. The next chapter, then, moves on to the group that all four radical right parties we have looked at so far sought to distance themselves from: Europe of Nations and Freedom.

5

# EUROPE OF NATIONS AND FREEDOM
## A MARRIAGE OF LOVE?

While European of Nations and Freedom (ENF) was the last of our three groups to be formed, on 16 June 2015, it was long in the making. Indeed, in some ways, its roots can be traced back to Jean-Marie le Pen's largely unsuccessful efforts to create radical right populist unity in the 1990s and 2000s (Startin 2010). As we discussed in Chapter 2, the failure of radical right populists in those decades to form a sole long-lasting European Parliament group, akin to those found among other party family types, was due to conflicting national interests, conflicting types of nationalism (ethnic vs. state), and fears about being tainted by association with one another (Fieschi 2000; Minkenberg and Perrineau 2007). Regarding the last point, we noted how, at different times, and according to their domestic goals, the leaders of the Dutch Partij voor de Vrijheid (PVV—

Party for Freedom), the Italian Lega Nord (LN—Northern League), and the Austrian Freiheitliche Partei Österreichs (FPÖ—Austrian Freedom Party) had disavowed any similarities to the French Front National (FN—National Front) and, in the case of the PVV, to both the FN and the FPÖ.

Yet, as Table 5.1 details, all these parties chose to sit together for the first time in the ENF group. So, what changed? Why did the LN (previously in the EFD with UKIP) and the PVV (which, as we saw in the last chapter, rejected the chance to join the EFD in 2011) opt to join former pariahs like the FN and VB?

Perhaps it is simply a story of policy congruence, as their common 'radical right' ideological denominator would suggest. But if it is, were they also policy congruent before, or does their alliance indicate that they moved closer on key issues after 2009? Leaving policy congruence aside, why were the previous obstacles to radical right populist co-operation, especially their fears of association with one another, no longer sufficient to keep these parties apart? After all, we know from the previous two chapters that the Danish People's Party, Finns Party, UKIP and Sweden Democrats preferred the ECR and EFDD due to concerns about the domestic effects of their European-level alliances. Why did the ENF parties act differently? And how have they squared Minkenberg and Perrineau's 'international group of nationalists' circle? In other words, how have they reconciled the strong defence and exaltation of their national interests and identities with their new international co-operation both inside and outside the European Parliament?

Table 5.1: Main members of ENF

| Party | Country | Vote in 2014 | MEPs in 2014 | Previous EP group |
|---|---|---|---|---|
| FN | France | 24.9 | 23* | NI |
| LN | Italy | 6.2 | 5 | EFD |
| FPÖ | Austria | 19.7 | 4 | NI |
| PVV | Netherlands | 13.3 | 4 | NI |
| VB | Belgium | 4.3 | 1 | NI |

Note: Votes in percentages. The number of MEPs given is those each party had at the first session of the new EP in July 2014.
* The FN lost several MEPs between the EP elections and the creation of the ENF in June 2015. The ENF also contained two Polish MEPs along with one from the UK. The total number of MEPs in the ENF when it formed was thirty-six.
Source: http://www.europarl.europa.eu/elections2014-results/en/election-results-2014.html; http://www.europarl.europa.eu/news/en/press-room/20150622IPR69217/opening-new-europe-of-nations-and-freedom-group-declared-formed

This chapter seeks to answer the questions above. It first discusses why the ENF's formation was delayed and how it eventually came about. We then look at Chapel Hill Expert Survey data to see the degree of policy congruence among the ENF parties. Given that we are interested in what changed, we compare their positions in

2009 and 2014 in order to see if they have moved closer together. We find that the parties have held broadly compatible positions on immigration, European integration, and social and economic left–right issues over the past decade. The creation of the ENF thus fits the 'policy congruence' theory, although, according to that theory the same parties should have allied previously, too. The positional fit in 2014 does not explain why they came together when they did. One change that the expert survey data does identify is the salience of these parties' opposition to European integration. This increased considerably between 2009 and 2014 for all the ENF parties, arguably making it more urgent and rational for them to band together. In other words, as we discuss also in the concluding chapter, there are now greater European-level reasons for radical right populist unity.

Our interview data builds on this. Between July 2014 and November 2018, we interviewed fourteen current and former MEPs, national-level MPs and key officials from the ENF parties who were able to shed light on the logics underpinning their parties' EP alliances and strategies.[1] These point us to several factors.

First, we note the importance of strong party leadership, and leadership change, in facilitating the creation of the ENF. Marine Le Pen's replacement of her father as FN leader in 2011 and subsequent process of *dédiabolisation* (de-demonisation) of her party was crucial in this respect, but the roles played by Matteo Salvini of the LN and Geert Wilders of the PVV were also very important. Second, we find that the ENF reflects the desire (long-held, in some cases) to create a lasting group made up of like-minded RRP parties which, unlike those we have discussed in the previous chapters, were unashamed of their commonalities with other radical right populists and unafraid of adverse domestic media reactions to their European partners. Finally, and linking back to the greater salience of European integration shown by our expert survey data, we find that the ENF parties see themselves now not only as defenders of their own nations, but also of a wider European (Christian) people against the threats posed by elites and 'others' (in particular, Islam). We argue therefore that these parties combine international populism, in which 'the people' is nation-based, and transnational populism, in which 'the people' is continental (Moffitt 2017: 410).

## *The delayed formation of the ENF*

At a press conference in The Hague on 13 November 2013, Marine Le Pen and Geert Wilders publicly announced their intention to form a group after the following year's European Parliament (EP) elections, prompting months of media headlines and speculation. This public event marked the culmination of a behind the scenes process that had begun many months earlier. As Ludovic de Danne, Marine Le Pen's main European advisor and a key architect of the eventual ENF, explained to us, Wilders had contacted them and they had 'a first lunch in Paris' in early 2013. The main function of this, De Danne said, was 'getting rid of false images' that each had about the other. As he put it, they had been 'inter-demonised' in the sense that Dutch and French media had given a distorted picture of each party to the other and so they needed to clarify their positions and views.

Vossen (2017: 78) says that, following this initial successful meeting, Wilders then 'trawled half of Europe in spring and summer 2013 in search of allies'. The tour included meetings with former Czech President Václav Klaus, Heinz-Christian Strache (leader of the FPÖ), Roberto Maroni (leader at the time of the Lega Nord), Jimmie Åkesson (leader of the Swedish Democrats), and Filip Dewinter and Gerolf Annemans (the first a leading figure, the second the leader at the time, of Vlaams Belang). According to Vossen (2017: 78–79), 'with the exception of Klaus, all were enthusiastic about the co-operation Wilders proposed. They all also welcomed Wilders as though he were a long-lost son'.

The month after the Hague press conference, Wilders, Annemans, Strache and De Danne spoke on behalf of their parties at the Lega Nord Congress in Turin.[2] This event marked the formal confirmation of Matteo Salvini as leader of the Lega Nord, following his resounding 82 to 18 per cent victory over the party's founder, Umberto

Bossi, in primary elections open to LN members (McDonnell and Vampa 2016: 110). More importantly for us, it also signalled the new international direction the Lega Nord would take under Salvini and underlined that these parties were not now afraid to be seen all together in public. As regards the themes of the speeches, Wilders predictably talked about Islam (saying 'no more Islam, no more Sharia, no more Mosques') and asserted 'we are patriotic people who want to fight for our own identity', while De Danne read a letter from Marine Le Pen in which she said 'I believe we can change the course of European history...we have a duty towards our people, our culture and our civilisation'.

The nascent radical right populist group initially operated under the name 'European Alliance for Freedom'. This was a Europarty, like the Alliance for Direct Democracy in Europe, mentioned in the previous chapter, that had been created in late 2010 and was formally recognised by the EP in 2011.[3] While membership of the EAF was, unusually, individual, it included leading figures from radical right populist parties like the Sverigedemokraterna (SD—Sweden Democrats), FPÖ, and FN, such as Kent Ekeroth (see Chapter 4), Marine Le Pen and the FPÖ MEP Andreas Mölzer. However, not all the parties of the EAF's individual members were likely to join Le Pen's group; for example, the EAF contained several current and former MEPs from UKIP. Although, as we noted in the previous chapter, the SD did meet Le Pen in the months before the election (Bolin 2015: 70–2) and the Slovenská Narodná Strana (SNS—Slovak National Party) expressed strong interest in joining, the core of the prospective EP group was made up of the five parties present at the Lega Congress: LN, FPÖ, FN, PVV and VB.

After the May 2014 European elections, those five core parties easily had the twenty-five MEPs required to create a group (see Table 5.1). But, since EP groups must also include MEPs from at least seven different member states, they were short of two country delegations. This was because, firstly, the Slovak National Party failed to gain any MEPs.[4] Secondly, and damningly, the Sweden Democrats decided to look elsewhere for EP alliances due to the perceived domestic costs of associating with parties like FN (see Chapter 4). As we have seen, having been swiftly rebuffed by the ECR, the SD ultimately joined the EFDD. There were no remaining viable options for the FN-led group among the five other radical right populist parties with MEPs in 2014. Three of these—the Danish People's Party, the Finns Party and UKIP—had all ruled out co-operation for the reputational reasons we have discussed previously. The other two, Jobbik from Hungary and the Kongres Nowej Prawicy (KNP—Polish Congress of the New Right), led by the extremely controversial Janusz Korwin-Mikke, were in turn considered untouchable by FN and its partners for similar reasons.[5]

One of the main people responsible for putting the group together, the (now former) FN MEP Aymeric Chauprade, told us in 2015: 'We could have made this group at the beginning, I was in charge of that. But Marine was very clear and she asked me to cut the relation with parties like Jobbik'. Likewise, as De Danne explained in 2014, shortly after their failure to form a group:

> If we had taken the Polish [KNP], we would not have been fair with our voters because we would have taken someone who is extremely radical when Marine Le Pen is doing all our efforts to get away from the radical elements of the past of the Front National.

The failure to form a group in 2014 was thus due to the same type of 'respectability' considerations that the parties discussed in the previous chapters had made about FN and FPÖ. FN continued to be shunned by some, but also shunned others much more than in the past. The key point, however, in understanding how the group was eventually created is that the toxicity of the KNP (as opposed to Jobbik) largely derived from its leader Korwin-Mikke, rather than the party, as De Danne's comment above about 'someone' underlines. This meant that when Korwin-Mikke was removed as KNP leader in January 2015, the possibility of including some of the party's other MEPs resurfaced. As Gerolf Annemans (MEP and former leader of the Vlaams Belang) explained in our interview, conducted on the day the ENF was launched in June 2015: 'We had long standing preparational talks with Polish friends that cleaned up their backyard, re-establishing the party without Mikke'. As a result, the KNP MEPs Stanisław Żółtek and Michał Marusik joined the new group. When asked whether Korwin-Mikke was completely out of the picture and would have no connection with the ENF, Annemans replied: 'Yes, that was a condition, of course'.

The seventh country delegation was provided by Janice Atkinson, a former UKIP MEP who had been expelled from UKIP in March 2015 following allegations concerning the misuse of expenses. According to Annemans, the suspension of Jean-Marie Le Pen from the FN in the weeks before the ENF was created and the consequent absence of him and Bruno Gollnisch from the EP group had 'helped a lot' to facilitate her entry.[6] While Atkinson, along with leaders and representatives of VB, FPÖ, FN, PVV and LN, was present at the press conference in Brussels that launched the ENF on 16 June 2015, the two KNP members were not.[7] Since all of the available evidence, including our interviews, indicates that the Polish MEPs played no significant role in the ENF other than helping the group to meet the country number requirement, we therefore do not discuss the KNP further in this book.

*The ENF: an ideologically homogenous group*

As we have already done for the ECR and EFDD, in this section we explore how well the ENF parties have fitted together on key policy dimensions. Given that we also want to investigate whether anything changed regarding policy positions that might explain the timing of the ENF parties' alliance, we have examined the CHES data for both 2009 and 2014. We will proceed in the same order as in the previous two chapters, examining first European integration, then immigration and, finally, social and economic left–right positions.

Figure 5.1: ENF parties 2009 and 2014, European integration

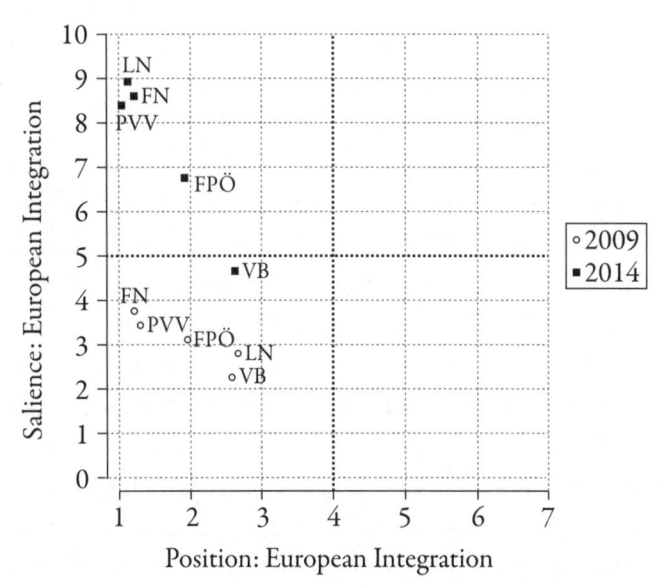

Source: Own calculations based on Chapel Hill Expert Survey data (Bakker et al. 2015).

Figure 5.1 shows the party positions and saliences regarding European integration in 2009 and 2014, with higher values denoting more supportive positions and higher saliences. We find that the five ENF parties are spread between negative positions around 3 to the very negative position of 1 (with a tendency towards the 'very negative' end of the scale). At the extreme, the PVV and FN are located constantly around the most negative position of 1 while the FPÖ is stable on a position of 2. The Lega Nord has moved from a less extreme negative position in 2009, to the extreme end in 2014. Only the VB remained, in both years, in more moderate positions between 2 and 3, which is understandable given that it is located in the country hosting the EU, with all the economic benefits that derive from that.[8]

Generally, the five parties are in consensus about their positions on European integration (standard deviation of 0.7 in both 2009 and 2014). The picture is slightly different for EU integration salience, which was low or moderate for all five parties in 2009—and they agreed broadly on this low salience (standard deviation of 0.6). We find a strong increase in salience in 2014, especially for the LN, FN and PVV. Because not all parties increased the salience to the same degree, we find a larger rise in the standard deviation to 1.8 and, thus, in heterogeneity in 2014. It is important to note, however, that the finding regarding salience is not specific to the ENF. If we compare the mean salience of all parties included in the CHES data set for 2009 and 2014, we find a general increase of salience from 2.8 (2009, N = 137) to 5.9 (2014, N = 122). Nonetheless, this increased salience might have been a facilitator for the formation of the ENF group as it made a strong unified Eurosceptic group a timelier project.

Table 5.2: Positions on immigration and deviation within ENF

| Year | VB | LN | FPÖ | FN | PVV | Deviation |
|------|-----|-----|-----|-----|-----|-----------|
| 2014 | 9.6 | 8.4 | 9.5 | 9.8 | 9.8 | 0.6 |
| 2009 | 9.7 | 9.9 | 9.3 | 9.7 | 9.9 | 0.2 |

Source: Own calculations based on Chapel Hill Expert Survey data (Bakker et al. 2015).

Table 5.2 shows the five parties' positions regarding immigration policy. As explained in previous chapters, higher values in the position scores mean that the parties prefer a more restrictive immigration policy, with 10 as the maximum. We find little change between 2009 and 2014 among the positions regarding immigration, with the parties consistently favouring very restrictive immigration policies. Table 5.2 also shows that the standard deviations between the party positions remained very low, indicating strong agreement. CHES experts were asked to evaluate the salience of immigration in the 2009 round of the survey, and to name the three most important policies for each party in the 2014 survey. In both measurements, immigration came out as extremely salient for the parties, being ranked on the salience scale between 8 and 10 in 2009 and as the most important issue in 2014 for all five main ENF parties. Hence, here too, we find generally strong agreement among these parties.

The situation regarding party positions on the generic economic and social left–right dimensions is slightly more mixed. Figure 5.2 shows that the ENF parties broadly occupied the upper-right corner of both economic and social right positions in 2009 and 2014. The largely empty figure underlines again how much these

Figure 5.2: ENF parties 2009 and 2014, left–right positions

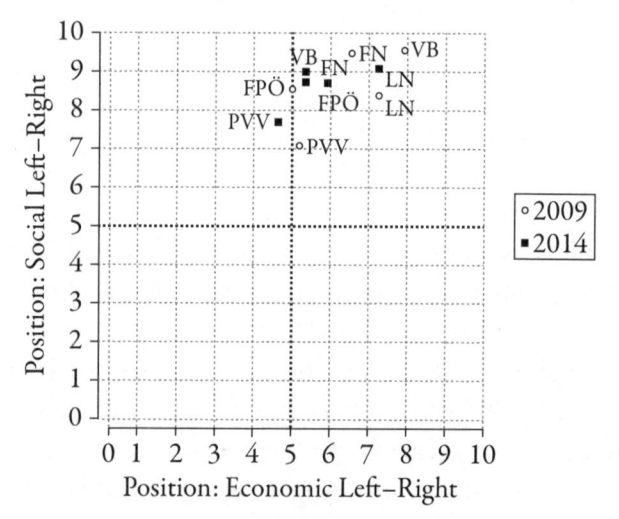

Source: Own calculations based on Chapel Hill Expert Survey data (Bakker et al. 2015).

parties cluster together. However, we also see more intra-group variation than on European integration or immigration. On the social dimension, all parties are located clearly in the conservative camp and the standard deviation between their position fell from 1.0 (2009) to 0.6 (2014). On the economic dimension we find some heterogeneity, with a decrease in the standard deviation from 1.3 (in 2009) to 1.0 (2014). The parties that now form the ENF have always held positions that are very close to at least some of the other member parties. Furthermore, the 2014 positions indicate a move to the left. In particular, both the PVV and the FPÖ crossed into the left space of the economic left–right dimension. These findings are in line with recent work that shows how radical right populist parties are increasingly adopting socio-economic positions to the left of their mainstream right-wing competitors (Roth et al. 2018).

The five main ENF parties thus appear in line with the dominant theory that parties with similar policy profiles form EP parliamentary groups. According to the CHES data, they are consistent in their positions and saliences on European integration and immigration, which are defining policies of contemporary radical right populist parties. While there is slightly more incongruence regarding the positions on the economic and social left–right dimensions, there is no obvious misfit on these aggregate positions, either. However, nothing in particular had changed regarding positions.

It is not that these parties became significantly more policy congruent after 2009 in a manner that would explain the timing of their alliance. As we have noted, the only significant difference between 2009 and 2014 was a shared increased salience of European integration, which perhaps provided a more prominent and urgent platform for co-operation.

## *ENF office spoils*

As regards the spoils of office that membership in an EP group offers, the situation is more clear-cut for most of the ENF parties than it was for the likes of the Danish People's Party and the Finns Party (see Chapter 3), which had a choice of groups in 2014 and had not been in the non-inscrits (NI—non-aligned) in previous legislatures. By contrast, the Front National, FPÖ, PVV and Vlaams Belang had all been in the NI since 2009. For these parties, the office advantage of the ENF is evident, as they gained access to greater funding, staffing and speaking time than they would have had in the NI. Of course, those same office benefits would have been available if they had formed a group during the 2009–2014 parliament, so office alone cannot explain why they created the ENF when they did.

In addition, while the extra funding and speaking time are no doubt welcome, the ENF parties seem to have followed the example of UKIP more than the

Danish People's Party in terms of their engagement with EP work, since none of their MEPs served as a chair or a vice-chair of an EP committee in the 2014–2019 parliament and they only held a handful of rapporteur positions (see Chapter 6). In other words, the ENF's representatives do not appear to have been particularly eager to take up the opportunities for greater parliamentary roles that group membership offered them.

Table 5.3: Financial resources per MEP, ENF and EFDD 2017

| Group | Year | MEPs* | EP Allocation, Euro | Per MEP, Euro |
|---|---|---|---|---|
| ENF | 2017 | 39 | 2,718,648.83 | 69,709 |
| EFDD | 2017 | 45 | 3,653,679.55 | 81,193 |

Notes: This does not take into account European party foundations contributions, donations, assets etc.
* Mid-year number of MEPs.
Sources: ENF 2018, p. 8; EFDD 2018, p. 9.

Table 5.3 shows the financial contributions to the END, made by the EP in 2017 and, for the sake of comparison, to the EFDD in the same year. As a slightly larger group, the EFDD got more, but nonetheless ENF parties gained access to funding levels comparable with those of a long-term radical right populist group member like UKIP. It is also noteworthy that resources for campaigning at the European level became available when the EU recognised the Europarty 'Movement for a Europe of Nations and Freedom' (MENF) in 2015.

MENF was founded by the main ENF parties in 2014 and was tightly linked to the ENF group. The available funding for MENF started out at 1,170,000 Euro in 2015 and increased annually (Directorate-General for Finance 2018). While the parliamentary group makes the foundation of a Europarty easier, because of the similarity in group size and composition requirements, the funds thereby available are not universally attractive to all parties. Notably, the Dutch PVV did not join the MENF.[9] The PVV was invited to the international congresses organised by MENF[10] but allegedly did not want to take European funds.[11]

## *The ENF: An idea whose time has come*

Other than the increased salience of European integration, if there were no significant policy positional changes, why did the five core ENF parties decide to form a group when they did? A first obvious explanation is that they (eventually) had the numbers to do so. Nonetheless, we know that previous attempts of the FN and VB to form groups with like-minded parties even when the required numbers might have been available either failed or did not last very long (Startin and Brack 2017: 30–37). We also know that the LN, the PVV and the FPÖ had—on specific occasions or consistently—shunned alliances with some or all of their ENF partners (especially FN) due to their fear of domestic audience costs (Fieschi 2000). So, if it is not a newfound policy convergence that brought about change or simply a question of numbers, how do we explain the creation of the ENF?

From our interviews with MEPs, MPs and senior advisors from the ENF parties, we can identify three main factors: (1) party leadership, especially the internal and external effects of leadership change in the Front National and Lega Nord, and the ability of radical right populist leaders like Le Pen, Salvini and Wilders to take and implement decisions swiftly and with little discussion; (2) the culmination of a long-held desire to move beyond fears of domestic audience costs deriving from each other's reputations and instead finally create a lasting international radical right populist group that is unashamed of its commonalities; (3) the re-casting of their mission as not just a series of national objectives, but a European goal. Let us take these three factors in order.

A new generation of party leaders

One of the ironies of the ENF is that, while it brings the long-held desire of Jean-Marie Le Pen for radical right populist unity to fruition, its creation is rooted in his 2011 resignation as FN leader and eventual suspension from the party in 2015. As we saw in the previous two chapters, any association with Le Pen Senior and, in particular, his anti-Semitism, remained in 2014 a strong deterrent for radical right populist parties like UKIP and the Danish People's Party. The new FN elites around Marine Le Pen were well aware of this. As Ludovic de Danne acknowledged, when discussing why the Sweden Democrats did not join the ENF: 'I think the reality is that they don't want to mix with Jean-Marie Le Pen'. Similarly, Aymeric Chauprade told us in 2015 that, because of the Le Pen name, 'some people are still afraid. They stay with the old perception of my party which was considered like a far-right party, but which is not the case actually, now'. For the other ENF parties however, the FN leadership change, and Marine Le Pen's subsequent attempt to detoxify the party's image, appears to have had a positive effect.[12]

Both Annemans of the VB and Johannes Hübner, FPÖ MP responsible for European and foreign policy, confirmed this. As the former put it: 'I join Marine Le Pen, not the father, to show you exactly what I mean'. While one could argue that the VB in particular had been close already to the FN in previous years, when Jean-Marie Le Pen was leader, the same could certainly not be said for Geert Wilders. As we noted in Chapter 2, the strongly pro-Israel PVV leader had previously repeatedly refuted any association with the anti-Semitic Jean-Marie Le Pen. Indeed, Vossen (2017: 77) notes the party's MEPs in the 2009–2014 EP were under orders not to appear near Jean-Marie Le Pen or Vlaams Belang representatives. As the former PVV MEP from 2009 to 2010, Louis Bontes recounts: 'We even had to change seats in parliament because old Le Pen sat a couple of seats behind us and we could easily have ended up in a photo together that way. Geert wouldn't allow that under any circumstances' (cited in Vossen 2017: 77).

According to former PVV MEP (2009–2014), Lucas Hartong, his leader's decision to pursue an alliance with Front National thus came as an unwelcome surprise to the party's MEPs, given both Wilders' previous position regarding the undesirability of EP alliances (see Chapter 4) and FN's bad reputation in the Netherlands.[13] Hartong told us how he sought to change Wilders' mind about teaming up with FN: 'I said 'please Geert, don't do this. It's not good for our party. It's not good for our voters in public perception, but also to reach our goals. It is so wrong to run with these people'. He didn't react'.

Wilders' lack of reaction likely reflects his iron control of the PVV, of which he is the only formal member and is, therefore, accountable only to himself (De Lange and Art 2011: 1240–41). Or, as Hartong put it, Wilders 'is the party'. Consequently, not only did he not have to consult about the new alliance but, as we have seen, he was able to act as its driving force in 2013 (Vossen 2017: 78).

If Wilders' control over the PVV helps to explain why it could change its stance on the FN and EP alliances so quickly and decisively, the same is true of Marine Le Pen's treatment of her own father. Having first suspended him from the party in May 2015, following (more) comments about the Holocaust, Marine Le Pen then led moves to abolish his position of honorary president and, finally, to expel him from the party. Discussing how Le Pen Junior has changed the party since taking over, Ivaldi and Lanzone (2016: 155) refer to a process of 'Marinisation' by which 'the FN continues to be organised around charismatic leadership with a weaker intermediary structure and a very strong central office'. This process has not only enabled Marine Le Pen to change positions quickly (e.g. regarding the Euro in 2017/18) but has also allowed her to side-line and then remove a major obstacle to co-operation with other radical right populist parties—her father.

Leadership change and the role of the leader are also important in explaining the Lega Nord's decision to join the ENF. While, as we noted earlier, Roberto Maroni met Wilders in the first half of 2013, it was at the end of that year, from the moment the new Lega Nord leader Matteo Salvini took over, that the party placed all its eggs in the future ENF's basket, inviting leading representatives from the other parties to speak at Salvini's first congress as leader in December. The LN did so despite the fact that, at the time, it was still formally part of the EFD group in the EP. Like Wilders, Salvini did not discuss the new alliance with most of his party's 2009–2014 MEPs. The LN delegation leader in that parliament, Francesco Speroni, explained to us in a

2014 interview: 'No, we were not consulted ... I was just presented with it as a decision, that's how it happened'. Nonetheless, Speroni recognised that joining parties like those in the ENF represented a better policy fit. He acknowledged: 'I had an excellent relationship with Nigel [Farage], but politically, we are much closer to FPÖ and so on'. Finally, as regards Salvini, it is worth noting that his replacement of the LN's regionalist, anti-centralist stance with an Italian nationalist, anti-Brussels position made it easier to ally with the strongly centralist and nationalist FN by removing the 'ethnic vs state nationalist' differences between the parties (Albertazzi et al. 2018). Again, the fact that Salvini has been able to change something that had been so fundamental to the Lega—its regionalism—indicates the very strong leadership he has been able to exert.

Proud populists

While party leadership changes and dynamics help to explain why the ENF alliance happened when it did, our interview data underlines how its creation reflects the culmination of a desire finally to create a durable international group of radical right populists that are proud to stand together and work towards common objectives. As we saw in Chapter 2, this had long been a goal of Le Pen senior and Gollnisch, but there were also figures in the other parties who had been working towards greater radical right co-operation in the years before the ENF's creation. Hence, while there may not have been formal links between some of the ENF parties before 2013, there were low-level international contacts based on, as Mudde (2007: 172) noted, 'personal relationships between leading party members in different countries'. In particular, the former MEPs Andreas Mölzer of the Austrian Freedom Party and Fiorello Provera of the Lega Nord had been active in attempts to counter what Mölzer described to us as the 'reciprocal marginalisation of the marginalised'.[14] He explained:

> These parties are isolated and labelled as 'extreme right' and, if they have contacts at European level, the establishment and media try to impede them by saying that the other parties of the democratic European right are 'extremist' or 'antidemocratic'. This strategy worked for a long time. Out of fear of being denigrated at home because of their collaboration with other parties, often contacts were dropped at European level. Interrupting this vicious cycle has always been a particularly important objective for me.

Provera expressed similar views, saying that his aim in quietly nurturing relations with what he saw as like-minded parties between 2009 and 2013 had been 'to finally bring out of isolation the various parties—Lega Nord, Front National, FPÖ, etc.—that get each labelled as xenophobic and racist parties'.[15] Their failure to co-operate on shared themes had been, in his view, due to their 'falling into the trap of left-wing political correctness', avoiding one another and therefore not speaking with one voice on issues such as immigration. He added, 'the left has been doing this forever. Think of the Socialist International, to name but one'.

These comments resonate with what we have seen in previous chapters. Many RRP parties have been wary—and some continue to be—of the domestic consequences of fraternising with similar parties from other countries (see also Startin and Brack 2017: 41). In 2014, parties like the Danish People's Party and the Sweden Democrats feared the perceptions of audiences in their countries (and especially the media) concerning the company they kept abroad. In particular, given their ambitions for national mainstream acceptance as potential partners in government, they sought to use their European affiliations to prove their domestic democratic credentials. They thus eschewed European policy congruence in favour of respectability, and participated in the 'marginalisation' of other radical right populists. To differing extents, this has historically also been true of the LN, PVV and FPÖ, when they have been in government and/or aspired to mainstream acceptance at home. For example, as we noted in Chapter 2, when the possibility of national office arose at the end of the 1990s, the FPÖ kept its distance from other RRPs in the EP, especially the FN (Fieschi 2000; Almeida 2010).

However, although both the FPÖ and LN in 2014 aspired to become parties of government again (and duly succeeded, in 2017 and 2018), they did not believe that co-operating with other radical right populist parties in Europe would be excessively costly in terms of national votes and/or office. The same calculation has obviously been made by Wilders. We see this as a 'coming of age' for such parties. In other words, rather than seeking to hide their similarities to other RRP parties and avoiding alliances for fear of media and other elite reactions, the ENF members are proudly part of a European radical right. Moreover, rather than seeing this partnership as a disadvantage in terms of their image, some view it as a positive. For example, Lorenzo Fontana, the former Lega Nord MEP (and, since 2018, a government minister), who claims to have introduced Salvini to Marine Le Pen, told us in 2015 that the ENF alliance was 'important for us, also as regards the media, to show there are people in Europe who think like us'. Similarly, when discussing the long-standing isolation imposed on his party through the *cordon sanitaire* in Belgium, Annemans of the VB said in 2015 that the ENF alliance means: 'All of a sudden we are amongst the biggest parties of other member states of which two or three are very strong and important member states in the European Union. It's a good thing for our image. It's an oxygen mask'.

Overall, the message we got from interviewees across the ENF parties was that they believed most media in their respective countries would criticise them whatever they did and that media reaction was therefore not a justification for continued avoidance of policy congruent alliances. It would require a separate study to examine how changing media structures and the fact that the public is less dependent on mainstream media for its political information are influencing radical right populist strategies, but they are surely relevant to some degree in explaining this attitude. Furthermore, given the opportunities offered by social media for political leaders and parties to communicate directly with voters (which Salvini and Wilders certainly do very well), some radical right populists may simply view old media as less relevant to disseminating their message (Van Kessel and Castelein 2016).

The fact that the ENF parties perceive image benefits from their alliance is underlined by the high-profile events they have organised outside the EP, such as their leaders' meetings in Milan in January 2016 and in Koblenz in January 2017 (see Chapter 6). Like our interviews, these events suggest that the ENF was not primarily designed to achieve specific EP objectives. The office benefits such as increased funding and speaking time were welcome, but—in contrast to our interviews with UKIP regarding what they themselves termed the EFDD's 'marriage of convenience'—the ENF was discussed by interviewees as an alliance that would persist beyond the 2014–2019 parliament, in terms of both length and scope. As the leader of the Vlaams Belang,

Tom van Grieken, told us in June 2015: 'I'm not personally interested in alliances for a short term, I only want a long-term alliance'.

Of course, not all radical right populists are 'proud populists' like those in the ENF. In particular, ENF interviewees referred to the refusal of the Sweden Democrats and UKIP to join them, attributing this to immaturity and excessive pragmatism in the first case and ego in the latter. As a leading FPÖ advisor commented to us in July 2014, regarding the SD:

> They think that if they are aligned to us it may cause a problem for them, for the upcoming elections for example ... We know that this is not the case. I mean, we know that if they're aligned, they will be attacked. If they are not aligned, they are also attacked, so we try to explain to them whatever you do they will not be different. But they are a young party. They have young people.

Annemans made a similar comment to us in 2014, which recalls the 'UKIP group as staging post' point we made in the previous chapter (and the metaphor by the UKIP official of how their group 'washed' parties that were trying to improve their image, like the DF and SD, and then set them off again on the road to respectability in the ECR). As Annemans put it, 'The EU-critical parties have a whitewash order: ECR upstairs, and then Farage between us, and then you see, that's a hierarchy of being whitewashed'. This metaphor appears to have been frequently used among radical right populists in the EP, since it was also referred to in our interviews with the FPÖ advisor and the Lega Nord's Fontana, who complained about 'this problem that some have, of trying to clean up their image, which was not even dirty in the first place!'

Regarding UKIP's refusal to countenance an alliance with FN, our ENF interviewees were all of the view that this was primarily about fear of damage to their image, as per our previous chapter, and personality. In particular, regarding the latter, they referred to the perceived reluctance of Farage to share the limelight with Marine Le Pen. The FN MEP, Nicolas Bay, told us in 2014, 'It's a question of leadership. Nigel Farage wants to have his own group in which he is the boss—and he has no desire to share the stage with a Front National party that is very strong. That's it, in a nutshell'. Or, as Annemans said of Farage and Le Pen when speaking to us in 2014: 'Him sitting two seats behind her? That's impossible'.

An international group of nationalists?

How has the ENF resolved the difficulties of maintaining an 'international group of nationalists' (Minkenberg and Perrineau 2007: 51), in light of its multiple national interests and identities? From our interviews, it emerges very clearly that this has not been a problem for the ENF parties. This is because, unlike UKIP, the ENF parties have been able to embrace a shared European identity alongside their various national identities. As the FN's

Aymeric Chauprade explained to us in 2015, 'Our position is clearly critical towards Europe and institutions. Not towards the European identity. We believe in the European identity'. Similarly, Fontana of the Lega Nord stated, 'We consider ourselves fully European. We believe that collaboration between European peoples is fundamental for the future'.

This collaboration is said to be increasingly important, even fundamental, due to twenty-first century threats to the peoples of Europe. Such threats are deemed to come not only from above, via national political elites and the bureaucrats of Brussels, but also from below: the ever-increasing presence of 'dangerous others' on a continental scale. In particular, the ENF parties have cast their co-operation as essential to protect the sovereignty, identity and security of (Christian) Europeans from secular and globalist elites, immigrants and, especially, Muslims. As the FPÖ European-level advisor told us: 'We are against the Islamisation of Europe ... we want to defend the identity, the cultures, the different languages, the different peoples of Europe'. Similarly, Chauprade explained:

> For us, 'to be' is more important than 'to have'. Of course, the economy is very important. We like reforms, we would like to transform the French economy to improve it. But the issue of the identity of France and the identity of Europe regarding the migrant problems, is something which is central.

The ENF thus recalls the efforts in previous decades of Jean-Marie Le Pen to foster a common European sense of belonging and mission among radical right populists (see Chapter 2). As he declared in a book published in 1984: 'We have expressed the wish to go beyond patriotism, beyond our respective feelings of national patriotism, to achieve a European patriotism' (Le Pen 1984: 163–64).[16] The ENF does indeed go beyond those 'respective feelings of patriotism'. If the Danish People's Party, Finns Party, UKIP and Sweden Democrats practiced solely what Moffitt (2017: 410) terms *international populism*, in which there are 'international ties between populist actors who are concerned with representing firmly nation-based conceptions of "the people"', we can say that the ENF parties have gone further by also espousing *transnational populism*, in which the people that populists appeal to and claim to speak for goes 'beyond the borders of the nation state'. Moreover, in line with populists' recourse to the language of 'crisis', they cast this European people as facing impending doom, with radical right populists as their only possible saviours. Or, as the FPÖ official put it to us:

> We think that we are the last hope of the people. Europe will fail. We will have a big problem in the end. There will be a collapse, whether it's the Euro or all this mass immigration. In 20 years, you will not recognise Europe anymore. That's what we think and so those parties we are talking about are the last hope of these

people. That's why we have to share our experience; we have to share our views and work together. This is our main goal. We don't care about having a little bit more money or resources.

## *Conclusion*

Unlike the long-standing groups containing other party families, there has never been a lasting EP group consisting entirely of radical right populist parties. Europe of Nations and Freedom (ENF) was designed to end that anomaly. Bringing together the Front National, Vlaams Belang, Austrian Freedom Party, the Italian Lega Nord and the Dutch Party for Freedom in a group for the first time, the ENF not only established a presence in the EP, but its core parties undertook a series of initiatives outside the parliament which indicate a long-term commitment (see Chapter 6). In this chapter, we have examined the drivers of this alliance and asked why it happened when it did, especially given the difficulties radical right populist parties have faced in the past in collaborating at European level.

Using CHES data, we showed that, while the main parties of the ENF were indeed very congruent in their main policies at the beginning of the 2014–2019 parliament, we do not see any significant change in this congruence compared to 2009. Similarly, while the spoils for EP groups were certainly an incentive for these parties to band together (given that four of them had previously been among the non-aligned), this incentive structure has not changed in a way that could explain the timing of the ENF formation.

In order to explore more deeply the reasons underpinning the group, we therefore analysed interviews with key figures from the ENF parties. These showed how the members of the ENF parties were aware that their European alliances might prompt negative feedback from national media. But rather than avoid this risk, they tried to break the vicious cycle of reciprocal demonisation and marginalisation. In this they have been assisted by the resignation, and then removal from his party, of one of the most controversial Western European politicians of recent decades—Jean-Marie Le Pen—and his replacement by Marine Le Pen. She has sought to move the FN's image away from associations with the extreme right and anti-Semitism (and away from her father). The very fact that parties such as the PVV and the LN have been willing to stand alongside the FN indicates that her *dédiabolisation* strategy has been at least partially successful at the European level. As we also argued, the strong control that Marine Le Pen, Geert Wilders and Matteo Salvini exerted over their respective parties in turn enabled them to make significant changes that facilitated their alliance quickly and decisively. Finally, our interviews revealed that the ENF represented the culmination of a long-term project on the far right. The ENF viewed itself as a lasting co-operation between defenders of European identity and values—just as Jean-Marie Le Pen had once envisaged. While still emphasising their respective national identities and sovereignty, the parties also make recourse to a broader notion of shared European identity that is under attack by both Brussels bureaucrats and non-natives, especially Muslims.

Thus, several aspects changed in 2014/2015. While radical right populists like the Danish People's Party and the Finns Party sought national legitimacy via EP alliances with mainstream parties in the ECR, parties like the PVV and Lega went in the opposite direction, towards radical right populists whom they had previously rejected. As we have seen, the ENF radical right populist group was made up of parties that were unashamed of their commonalities and could sit together, just as other established ideological party types do. This normalisation (or 'coming of age') of party behaviour might also have been aided by the fact that, in the aftermath of the 2015 European refugee crisis, the core issue of these parties—immigration—increased in importance. Moreover, it is an issue perceived by both electorates and parties not so much as a pressing 'national' question threatening native wellbeing, but as a 'European' issue—and a primarily European problem requires European solutions. In that sense, as we will discuss in greater depth in the concluding chapter, the ENF is incentivised to espouse not just international populism, but transnational populism.

6

# RADICAL RIGHT POPULISTS INSIDE AND OUTSIDE THE EUROPEAN PARLIAMENT

The last three chapters have discussed the different logics underpinning radical right populist participation in three European Parliament (EP) groups formed in 2014 and 2015: European Conservatives and Reformists (ECR), Europe of Freedom and Direct Democracy (EFDD) and Europe of Nations and Freedom (ENF). We saw that the four radical right populist parties in the ECR and EFDD disdained European-level policy congruence in favour of domestic respectability and audience costs considerations. The Dansk Folkeparti (DF—Danish People's Party) and the Finnish Perussuomalaiset (PS—Finns Party) were motivated primarily by the perceived benefits of 'respectable marriages' in the EP with mainstream parties, although they did also share Euro-critical interests and a desire to engage in legislative decision-making with their fellow ECR members. While UKIP and the Sverigedemokraterna (SD—

Sweden Democrats) similarly took into account the national-level consequences of associating with other radical right parties, the EFDD appeared different to the ECR in that it was conceived of as primarily a marriage of convenience through which parties could access office benefits without having expectations of policy alignment or parliamentary group loyalty imposed upon them. Finally, the ENF was the only homogenous radical right populist group whose parties conformed to the 'policy congruence' thesis and presented themselves as an ideologically cohesive union of like-minded parties who were now unashamed of their commonalities.

Having joined their various groups, what did radical right populist parties then do in the 2014–2019 EP? Did they vote together with their partners? Did the groups have a life beyond parliament? How did radical right populists use their EP affiliations at national level? Did they remain in the same groups for the duration of the parliament? If not, why not? Given the different motivations for their affiliations, we would expect radical right populists in the three groups to pursue different types of behaviour inside and outside the EP. In particular, given what interviewees told us (see Chapter 4), we would not expect the members of the EFDD's loose alliance to co-operate with each other in the same ways as parties in the ECR and ENF. The ECR representatives we spoke to, both radical right populist and mainstream, claimed they were committed to pursuing their Euro-critical positions through parliamentary work, while the ENF parties were of course closely aligned on their key issues. We would therefore expect parties in these groups to maintain cohesion within parliament. As regards their external actions and profiles, we would imagine that the Danish People's Party and the Finns Party publicised their participation in the ECR—and especially their partnership with the UK Conservatives—to domestic audiences, given their 'respectable marriage' reasons for moving to the ECR. Similarly, we would envisage that the ENF parties communicated their common ideology, strength, unity and shared purpose to their publics. Finally, given the fluidity and precarious history of EP groups on the right, we would expect to see a reasonable degree of movement in and out of the groups over the course of the legislature.

In this chapter, therefore, we look at what happened after the formation of the ECR, EFDD and ENF, in order to understand the stability and coherence of these groups in the 2014–2019 parliament and their utility for radical right populists. For the most part, we find that they behaved in ways consistent with what we have seen in the previous three chapters. Using VoteWatch roll-call voting data, we show that all three groups were less cohesive than other EP groups, but that the EFDD was particularly divided. Similarly, while EFDD parties like UKIP and the PVV in the ENF had little interest in taking on rapporteur positions within the parliament, this was more important for the Danish People's Party in the ECR. As regards their behaviour outside the EP, we see from the parties' national press releases that none has particularly used their EP group membership in general election campaigns since 2014. However, and in line with their 'proud populists' image, the ENF ran a series of high-profile events featuring their party leaders, which seemed designed to gain national and international media attention. Finally, we see that only the Sweden Democrats made a significant move out of their original group, switching from the EFDD to the ECR in July 2018. As our interviews show, this was entirely in line with the party's long-term 'respectability' goals and also fits the 'staging post' view of the EFDD discussed in Chapter 4.

*Voting together in Parliament*

Group cohesion means that MEPs within a group vote together, maximising their group's weight and communicating a picture of unity. The cohesion of EP groups grew steadily between 1979 and 2001, in parallel with the growth of EP powers (Hix et al. 2005). The ideological closeness of the parties within a group plays a major role in cohesion. Several studies have shown that the more parties in a group agree on their overall ideology, as well as specific policy issues, the more cohesively the group behaves in the EP (Hix et al. 2005, 2007; Bressanelli 2012; Whitaker and Lynch 2014). At the same time, the effectiveness of the groups themselves plays a central role in cohesion and they generally have a disciplinary effect on their MEPs (Hix et al. 2005: 231). Hix et al. (2007) find evidence for the hypothesis that larger groups have more potential influence on the EP's legislative process and thus exert a stronger disciplining effect on their members than smaller groups.

If these logics hold for the three groups containing radical right populists in the 2014–2019 EP, we would expect the ECR, as the third largest group in the EP, to be one of the most cohesive groups after the two main ones: the (mostly) centre-right European People's Party (EPP) and the (mostly) centre-left Socialists and Democrats group (S&D). By the same token, we would expect there to be less cohesion among the smaller EFDD, especially since we know from our interviews and other studies that its largest member, UKIP, was largely uninterested in the legislative process (e.g. Brack 2017a; Whitaker and Lynch 2014). Finally, as the ENF was the smallest group, we would also expect less cohesion among its members if we only take its potential influence in the EP into account. However, given that the ENF presented itself as an ideologically tightly knit group with a common purpose, we would envisage greater coherence from it than the EFDD, in order to showcase the parties' shared ideology and newfound unity.

We have investigated the cohesion of the three groups using roll-call vote data from more than four years, between 1 July 2014 and 4 October 2018,[1] obtained from the VoteWatch (votewatch.eu) platform. Roll call votes in the European Parliament are those decisions where every MEP present in the EP publicly declares their vote ('yes', 'no', or 'abstain'). Figure 6.1 shows the cohesion of the EP groups since 2014 (and 2015 in the case of the ENF). The line indicates that the average cohesion for groups was 80.7 per cent. In other words, the parties in EP groups vote together in four out of five legislative decisions. The figure also shows clearly that the three groups with radical right populist parties have lower cohesion scores than all other groups. As we expected, the EFDD has the lowest score of the three since its MEPs vote together only 50 per cent of the time. However, the fact that the ENF votes together in only 75 per cent, and the ECR in 78 per cent of roll-call votes them is less than we expected. In other words, notwithstanding the link between size and voting cohesion, the ECR is less cohesive than smaller EP groups such as GUE-NGL and Greens/EFA.

Table 6.1 provides a more detailed picture of the three groups' cohesion, breaking down the statistics by policy area. It shows the EFDD has very little internal discipline, with no policy area clearly countering the trend of group division. Its highest area of cohesion is with regards to the internal regulations of the EP, but even here the group only votes together two-thirds of the time. This finding is in line with the low cohesion noted by Whitaker and Lynch (2014: 246–7) in UKIP's previ-

Figure 6.1: Group cohesion in the EP 2014–2018

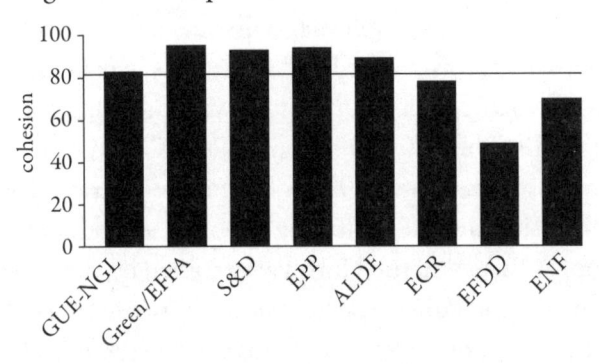

[Bar chart showing cohesion values for groups GUE-NGL, Green/EFFA, S&D, EPP, ALDE, ECR, EFDD, ENF]

Note: Groups are listed from left to right, broadly reflecting their ideology rather than size.
Source: Own calculation, based on Votewatch data.

ous group, the EFD. We also know from our interviews that the EFDD parties tended not to meet all together to co-ordinate their positions. The MEP Petr Mach, from the Czech Party of Free Citizens, told us in 2015 that, while the Sweden Democrats, like him, regularly attended UKIP's pre-vote meetings, the Five Star Movement (M5S) 'have their own meetings on how to vote'. In line with what we saw in Chapter 4, this did not pose a problem for any of our UKIP or Five Star Movement interviewees. As the M5S MEP Ignazio Corrao told us in 2015, beyond their criticism of the governance of the EU, 'we are in total disagreement with UKIP and the other members of our group. You can see this objective reality by looking at the voting results'.

The ECR and ENF have higher cohesion scores than the EFDD, but are still markedly less cohesive than all other EP groups. In the ECR's case, this may be because it has two ideological subgroups, with more mainstream parties like the UK Conservatives and Czech Občanská demokratická strana (ODS—Civic Democratic Party) on one side and the radical right populists of the Danish People's Party and the Finns Party, joined by the strongly right-moving Polish Prawo i Sprawiedliwość (PiS—Law and Justice), on the other (Stanley and Cześnik 2019). The likelihood of this being the source of voting division is supported by the fact that the ECR policy areas with the least cohesion are the highly value-driven culture and education ones, as well as gender equality, while the highest cohesion is in legal affairs and a range of economic policy areas.

The low coherence of the ENF is also surprising, given that the group is ideologically homogenous and the parties generally agree on policy priorities (see Chapter 5). As the French Front National (FN—National Front), the Freiheitliche Partei Österreichs (FPÖ—Austrian Freedom Party), the Belgian Vlaams Belang (VB—Flemish Interest), the Dutch Partij voor de Vrijheid (PVV—Party for Freedom) and the Italian Lega Nord (LN—Northern League) are all clear radical right populist parties, immigration, national culture and Euroscepticism are high on their agenda. However, even in the policy areas that affect these issues, like civil

Table 6.1: Group cohesion by policy area

|  | ECR | EFDD | ENF | *Average of all other EP groups* |
|---|---|---|---|---|
| All policies | 77.7 | 48.1 | 69.2 | 90.3 |
| Agriculture | 64.3 | 37.5 | 58.9 | 87.4 |
| Budget | 71.0 | 59.5 | 72.8 | 89.1 |
| Budgetary control | 85.2 | 56.7 | 73.3 | 93.5 |
| Civil liberties, justice & home affairs | 73.0 | 38.9 | 72.6 | 91.1 |
| Constitutional & inter-institutional affairs | 76.2 | 54.2 | 72.9 | 89.3 |
| Culture & education | 63.6 | 47.7 | 69.8 | 93.2 |
| Development | 77.6 | 39.0 | 66.2 | 92.9 |
| Economic & monetary affairs | 85.1 | 54.7 | 61.8 | 91.9 |
| Employment & social affairs | 77.6 | 36.8 | 72.5 | 90.1 |
| Environment & public health | 75.8 | 41.1 | 70.7 | 89.7 |
| Fisheries | 72.6 | 48.9 | 62.9 | 86.5 |
| Foreign & security policy | 81.1 | 49.0 | 67.9 | 89.7 |
| Gender equality | 64.0 | 33.4 | 69.2 | 89.4 |
| Industry, research & energy | 84.5 | 44.6 | 65.7 | 89.8 |
| Internal market & consumer protection | 87.1 | 46.6 | 69.5 | 90.5 |
| Internal regulations of the EP | 74.3 | 68.7 | 73.5 | 89.4 |
| International trade | 87.0 | 50.3 | 71.2 | 90.6 |
| Legal affairs | 87.6 | 47.0 | 65.1 | 92.4 |
| Petitions | 55.2 | 42.7 | 64.4 | 92.9 |
| Regional development | 73.4 | 45.5 | 66.9 | 94.7 |
| Transport & tourism | 75.8 | 43.3 | 66.1 | 87.5 |

liberties, justice and home affairs, or culture and education, the ENF acts cohesively in only 70 per cent of votes. Since the cohesion within the policy areas ranges between 59 and 74 per cent, there are no specific topics that stand out as being of more or less importance. Thus, given the high policy congruence between the national parties that work together in the ENF, the main explanation for this low voting congruence must be a lack of will, or ability, to discipline the voting behaviour of the group's members (see Hix et al. 2005). Finally, it is also worth noting that the ECR, EFDD and ENF did not tend to vote together as a 'right-wing Eurosceptic bloc'. Although commentators and journalists had hypothesised before the 2014 elections about the effects of such a bloc on the parliament's work and the EU's policy agenda, it did not come to pass.[2] The ENF and EFDD voted together in 49 per cent of votes, the EFDD and ECR in 44 per cent, and the ENF and ECR in just 39 per cent.

Table 6.2 gives more information and explanation for what happened within the three groups as it shows the loyalty of the parties to the groups. Loyalty is defined by calculating, for each vote, whether the vote of the plurality in a national party delegation ('yes', 'no' or abstention) matches the political line of the EP group as a whole. If it does, then that national party delegation is considered 'loyal', otherwise it is considered 'rebel'. Table 6.2 shows that parties are on average loyal to their

EP groups in 91 per cent of all decisions. Within the various groups, largest parties have the highest loyalty, which makes sense as they are most likely to influence the group decision.

Table 6.2: Loyalty of individual parties to groups

| *Group* | *Party* | *Country* | *MEPs*[*] | *Loyalty* |
|---|---|---|---|---|
| all | | | 732 | 91% |
| ECR | PS | Finland | 2 | 96% |
| | Conservatives | UK | 20 | 91% |
| | ODS | Czechia | 2 | 86% |
| | PiS | Poland | 14 | 85% |
| | DF | Denmark | 3 | 79% |
| EFDD | UKIP | UK | 22 | 77% |
| | SD | Sweden | 2 | 71% |
| | M5S | Italy | 17 | 51% |
| ENF | Front National[**] | France | 22 | 85% |
| | Vlaams Belang | Belgium | 1 | 59% |
| | Lega Nord | Italy | 5 | 56% |
| | PVV | Netherlands | 4 | 52% |
| | FPÖ | Austria | 4 | 49% |

Notes: No data for SD in ECR because of short time frame.

[*] Number of MEPs in groups at beginning of EP session.

[**] Weighted average for Front National (twenty MEPs), Front National/ Rassemblement Bleu Marine (one) and Rassemblement Bleu Marine (one).

The most interesting finding in Table 6.2 concerns the ENF. As we have seen, this group is ideologically very congruent on those policy issues that are defining for radical right populist parties, but has slightly less congruence with regards to general economic policies (see Chapter 5). The FN, being by far the largest ENF party in terms of MEPs, comes out as most loyal. This is likely caused by its domination of decisions on the group's positions. Nonetheless, it is surprising to find that the smaller parties only vote with the ENF group in 50–60 per cent of legislative decisions, which is at a similar level to the EFDD. This suggests to us that, while the ENF portrays itself as a coming together of like-minded parties, so far they either simply disagree with one another on more issues than we might have expected, or they continue to let specific national interests trump those of European-level loyalty. Or, most plausibly, they simply do not care enough about EP legislative work to bother co-ordinating positions and enforcing group voting discipline.

## *Parliamentary roles by radical right populist MEPs*

Another facet of the legislative engagement of parties and groups in the EP is the extent to which their MEPs become rapporteurs. Rapporteurs take the lead in drafting and negotiating specific legislation within parliamentary committees, and this gives them a central and powerful position within the legislative process. If the committee that allocates a rapporteur is the principal committee in the matter, the rapporteur takes the lead on drafting the legislative act and creates a report. The rapporteurs of other participating committees write recommendations. Depending on size, each EP group receives a number of points with which they can bid for rapporteur positions: the subsequent allocation of these positions is an intra-group decision.

Table 6.3 shows all the rapporteur positions that the main parties in the ECR, EFDD and ENF held between July 2014 and February 2019 as well as in any legislative processes in progress at the time of the data collection. The results are in line with our earlier discussions, in Chapters 3 and 4, about the differing importance of EP legislative work for parties. We can see in Table 6.3 that, in the ECR, this was dominated by the UK Conservatives and, to a lesser degree, the Polish PiS. The two reports from the Finns Party were both drafted by Jussi Halla-Aho and are on regulations regarding third party nationals, how they are allowed to settle within the EU, and how they should be removed from the EU.

In relation to their small group size, the Danish People's Party held a large number of rapporteur offices in the 2014–2019 parliament. Each of their three MEPs was a rapporteur at least once and the policy areas are widely spread. In our interviews with DF representatives, they pointed to the value of these roles for their image. For example, when we spoke to him in 2018, Morten Messerschmidt commented that 'It was hugely

Table 6.3: Rapporteurs 2014–2019

|  | No. MEPs** | Reports Nr | Reports MEPs | Recommendations Nr | Recommendations MEPs | Opinions Nr | Opinions MEPs | WiP* Nr | WiP* MEPs |
|---|---|---|---|---|---|---|---|---|---|
| ECR |  |  |  |  |  |  |  |  |  |
| UK Conservatives | 19 | 27 | 12 | 3 | 1 | 32 | 11 | 10 | 4 |
| PiS | 18 | 12 | 5 | 0 | 0 | 12 | 5 | 7 | 4 |
| DF | 3 | 6 | 3 | 2 | 2 | 2 | 2 | 0 | 0 |
| ODS | 2 | 2 | 2 | 1 | 1 | 4 | 2 | 4 | 1 |
| PS | 2 | 2 | 1 | 0 | 0 | 0 | 0 | 0 | 0 |
| SD*** | 2 | 0 | 0 | 0 | 0 | 0 | 0 | 0 | 0 |
| EFDD |  |  |  |  |  |  |  |  |  |
| UKIP | 20**** | 0 | 0 | 0 | 0 | 2 | 1 | 0 | 0 |
| M5S | 14 | 37 | 12 | 3 | 1 | 36 | 11 | 21 | 9 |
| SD | 2 | 1 | 1 | 0 | 0 | 0 | 0 | – | – |
| ENF |  |  |  |  |  |  |  |  |  |
| FN | 15 | 5 | 1 | 0 | 0 | 2 | 1 | 3 | 1 |
| LN | 6 | 2 | 1 | 1 | 1 | 0 | 0 | 1 | 1 |

| | | | | | | | | |
|---|---|---|---|---|---|---|---|---|
| FPÖ | 4 | 4 | 1 | 0 | 5 | 2 | 1 | 1 |
| PVV | 4 | 0 | 0 | 0 | 0 | 0 | 0 | 0 |
| VB | 1 | 0 | 0 | 0 | 1 | 1 | 0 | 0 |

Notes: as of group composition 27 February 2019.

\* Work in Progress: ongoing legislative processes in February 2019 with rapporteurs from ECR (forty-seven), EFDD (twenty-six) and ENF (six). Those WiP not accounted for in the table have rapporteurs from amongst the other (mainly independent) MEPs in the groups.

\*\* Number of MEPs in February 2019.

\*\*\* Sweden Democrats since their switch to ECR in July 2018.

important for us, as soon as possible after the elections in 2014, that I had a rapporteurship to prove that now we were working in the process, and so on'. Indeed, such was its importance that when the party had an internal discussion over whether Messerschmidt should withdraw his name from a competition policy report which contained a number of parts that the DF opposed, they concluded that:

> The very position of being a rapporteur and saying, 'This is a Messerschmidt report' and of course, there were areas where we could say, 'This is our fingerprint' and so on, were of such importance that we kept it. It gave a sense of seriousness, that we were not only there for opposition.

The situation for the radical right populists in the EFDD is very different. Table 6.3 shows clearly the Italian Five Star Movement taking up most of the positions in the legislative process that the EFDD could fill, in line with what we learned from our interviews, in Chapter 4. Given that M5S only ever had at most seventeen MEPs during the period, the fact it held the leading position in specific legislative processes more than seventy times suggests a party punching well above its weight. UKIP and SD, however, were largely inactive and did not take up any notable legislative positions. The two opinions from UKIP were drafted by William, Earl of Dartmouth and concerned the EU's 2019 draft general budget[3] while the sole report from the Sweden

Democrats was drafted by Peter Lundgren and covered a directive on driving licences.[4]

Finally, Table 6.3 shows there has been little take-up of rapporteur positions among the ENF parties. As a point of reference, 569 legislative process were in progress at the time of our data collection (Feb 2019) and ENF parties were only involved in five of them as rapporteurs. Within the parties, such work was overwhelmingly undertaken by specific MEPs. This trend was most pronounced in Front National, where only one MEP (Gilles Lebreton) served as rapporteur and all five of his reports were about the parliamentary immunity of other (non-FN) MEPs. With the exception of the Lega Nord, which at the time of data collection had fewer MEPs and therefore positions compared to the 2009–2014 EP, the ENF parties have all gained some form of office through rapporteur positions compared to the previous legislature, but the numbers are very small and it seems these roles are not of great importance to the parties.

## ECR, EFDD and ENF in the national arena

One means that parties have of making the EP group meaningful, beyond sitting together in Brussels and Strasbourg, is by seeking to deploy supranational alliances to their advantage at the national level. For example, in general election campaigns, radical right populists may use their EP group affiliations to show domestic elites and publics that they are accepted and valued by other parties in Europe. We would expect to see this particularly in the case of the Finns Party and the Danish People's Party, whose representatives told us that being associated with the UK Conservatives in Europe would help them at home. But it could also apply to parties like the Sweden Democrats, whose alliance in 2014 with UKIP rather than the Front National was intended to send domestic audiences a message about their legitimacy and direction of travel. Indeed, even for the Front National, the mere fact of having any parties willing to sit alongside them at length in the EP is a novelty and could be publicised as an indication that Marine Le Pen's 'de-demonisation' strategy is working and that the party's views are shared by other successful European parties like the Italian League and the Austrian Freedom Party.

To investigate whether, and how, radical right populists in the European Parliament deployed their group memberships in communications during general election campaigns, we analysed the press releases and, where possible, news items gathered from the parties' webpages. We collected press releases directly from the party webpages for the six-month period before all relevant general elections that took place during the 2014–2019 EP. We were able to gather this data for the Austrian FPÖ, the French Front National, the Italian Lega and the Dutch PVV from the ENF; UKIP and the Sweden Democrats from the EFDD; and the Finns Party from the ECR.[5] We analysed the press releases by counting the occurrence of key words that would indicate the use of the EP alliances during the campaign, i.e. the EP group names, the names of the other parties in the respective group and the names of other parties' leaders.

Table 6.4 shows the results of this analysis. We can see that radical right populist parties do not seem to mention their EP groups, or their fellow group members, in general election campaigns. The only exceptions are the Finns Party and, to a lesser extent, the Sweden Democrats once they moved to the ECR in July 2018. A closer look at the Finns' press releases reveals that their mentions are mainly of the other Nordic radical right populist parties. They refer to the Sweden Democrats twenty-five times in 2014/15 even though they were not yet in the same group. They also report that Morten Messerschmidt (DF) visited and they praised him for his 'strong personal charisma and great speech skills' (6 February 2015). Similarly, the Sweden Democrats only mention the ECR and the UK Conservatives when they announce they have been accepted as a member, and do not do so thereafter. Instead, they underline their close co-operation with the Danish People's Party and Finns Party, which seems to be based mainly on their shared Nordic character.

Table 6.4 also shows that, despite their claims of being a tight-knit group, the main ENF parties did not use this connection in their national press releases. Neither the Austrian Freedom Party nor the Northern League mention the group or its members at all in their respective general election campaigns of 2017 and 2018.[6] Press releases by the Dutch PVV only mention the ENF once, referring to an episode when Wilders was a guest at the meeting of ENF parties and the AfD in Koblenz (Germany) on 21 January 2017. The Front National refers to the FPÖ once, in December 2016 when discussing the 'tremendous thrust of the FPÖ in Austria' as an example of 'the global rejection of all policies of the European Union, economic and migratory in particular [that] is accelerating on the continent'. However, in general, neither they nor the other ENF members name-dropped their partners in press releases as much as we envisaged.

Another way for parties to make use of their EP affiliations at national level is to stage events together and/or have representatives from their European partners speak at election events. To see if this happened, we did an online search for all ECR, EFDD and ENF MEPs to investigate whether since July 2014 they had (a) appeared in specifically group-related events or (b) campaigned in the general elections of their group allies. For each search with the combination [MEP name + EP group + event], we noted the type of event, date, other MEPs present and the source of information. We did this for MEPs in the three groups as of January 2019, and only included events

Table 6.4: Press release analysis, six months before national election

|  | ENF | | | | EFDD | | ECR | |
|---|---|---|---|---|---|---|---|---|
|  | FPÖ | FN | PVV | LN | UKIP | SD | Finns | SD[b] |
| Time frame | April 17–Oct 17 | Nov 16–May 17 | Sept 16–March 17 | Sept 17–March 18 | Dec 16–June 17 | March 18–July 18 | Nov 14–April 15 | July 18–Sept 18 |
| N | 406 | 279 | 20 | 196 | 259 | 70 | 433 | – |
| Mentions |  |  |  |  |  |  |  |  |
| EP group Parties in | 0 | 0 | 1 | 0 | 2[a] | 0 | 33 | 3[a,b] |
| EP group Leaders in | 0 | 1 | 4[a] | 0 | 0 | 0 | 5 | 12[b] |
| EP group | 0 | 0 | 4[a] | 0 | 0 | 0 | 3 | 1 |
| EP voting | 2 | 2 | 0 | 0 | 3 | 3[a] | 3[a] | 0 |

Notes: [a] Same press release. [b] SD moved from EFDD to ECR in July 2018.

that took place outside the EP itself. Furthermore, we collected all major events organised by the three groups' Europarties: the Alliance of Conservatives and Reformists in Europe (ACRE—Europarty of ECR); the Alliance for Direct Democracy in Europe (ADDE—Europarty of EFDD, closed down in 2016 after financial irregularities); and Movement for a Europe of Nations and Freedom (MENF—Europarty of ENF).

The results of this analysis show clear differences between the three groups. Of the seventy-eight MEPs that are were part of the ECR, we could not find any group-related events for fifty MEPs. For the four and a half years in our search frame, we found thirteen minor and fringe events, with only two or three MEPs present. Although specifically branded with the 'ECR' name, most events involving the group's radical right populists would have had at best localised attention. For example, Timo Soini, leader of the Finns Party at the time, spoke twice at a UK Conservative fringe meeting organised by the ECR in November 2014.[7] We only found one major event with activities involving a larger number of ECR MEPs. This was at the annual four-day UK Conservative Party conference in September/October 2018, which included a series of events hosted by the ECR discussing the UK and the EU's future security and economic relationship. Amongst the participants was the Danish People's Party MEP Anders Vistisen.[8] Similarly, ACRE, the Europarty connected to the ECR, rarely had large-scale engagement outside Brussels. In 2015 and 2016, only project meetings took place, while 2017 saw the Great Lakes Trade Summit in Kampala and the Yerevan summit. Summits in 2018 were located in places like Baku (Azerbaijan) and Orhei (Moldova) and the only event to take place within the EU was the presentation in Luxembourg of the group's 2019 *Spitzenkandidat*, Jan Zahradil, from the ODS.[9] Thus, while the ECR organised events at the national level, these were infrequent and seem to have been relatively small affairs.

How can we reconcile this disparity between the importance of ECR membership for their national image, which the Danes and Finns mention in our interviews, with their apparent lack of efforts to publicise this at national level? One explanation might be that the point of their EP group choice is primarily to send messages to domestic political, media and economic elites about their 'respectability' (and suitability for government) rather than directly to the wider public. This would fit with the fact that, in our interviews, subjects from the two parties acknowledged that there is very little awareness, not only among the public but even among their party at grassroots level, of the EP group they sit in. As the DF's Vistisen told us in 2014 about his party's ordinary members: 'Most of them didn't know we were sitting in the EFD before, and most of them will not know that we are in the ECR now'. When we spoke to him again three years later, he was of the same view, but made a distinction for their partnership with the UK Conservatives. Referring to the general public, he said, 'They don't know anything about the ECR group. They will not be able to mention that, but what they might know because we tell them quite a lot, is that we are affiliated with the Tories'. He explained the way the DF sought to make domestic capital from its EP affiliation as follows:

> You're not trying to lift the ECR platform. We're just saying we are in the family of the Tories, of the British Conservatives. And you know, there are some very good brands there, primarily Thatcher and Churchill. Everyone knows those figures, they are internationally known. And that is how we are using it. We are not using it as the ECR.

The leading DF MEP Morten Messerschmidt made a similar point regarding the importance of the public and grassroots members associating his party with well-known foreign political figures, rather than a little-known European Parliament group. Discussing group-branded events, he told us in 2018:

> It's more if you have individuals that people know. For instance, in our annual convention of the party in, I think, 2011 or 2012, it was originally decided that Timo Soini should come and give a speech and there were some difficulties in his party, so he cancelled on the very day or the day before and I called Nigel [Farage] and he came. And that was hugely popular.

> People could actually see this guy that they knew from YouTube and so on, but it was not the EFD or the ECR or whatever. It's not the group as such.

While Farage may have been willing to do this type of work with his partners in the EFD, the situation in the EFDD seems to have been different, as the level of group-based engagement at national level is virtually non-existent. We found eighteen Brexit-related events that were branded as EFDD events, but these only included UKIP MEPs and all took place in the UK. We also found three small events that included a lone UKIP MEP and one other EFDD MEP, but no major events. The activities of the Europarty connected to the EFDD, the Alliance for Direct Democracy in Europe (ADDE), are necessarily curtailed as this organisation was only recognised by the EP in 2015, and was then closed down after a financial audit in 2016. The activities of ADDE, while it was still in existence, were restricted to Brexit-related events featuring Nigel Farage and other UKIP MEPs, flash visits by its members (e.g. to Macedonia in October 2015), and participation in the Jerusalem Leaders' Summit in 2015.[10]

While the ECR held small events at the national level and the EFDD did not really engage in such activities at all, the ENF approach was markedly different. While most of the group's relatively unknown MEPs did not take part in ENF-specific events, the group and its Europarty focused on large conferences and rallies that brought together their party leaders. To take a few examples: in July 2016, Marine Le Pen, Heinz-Christian Strache and representatives of the LN and the AfD encouraged the British people to vote for Brexit during an event called 'Patriotic Spring' that was held in Vienna.[11] The following January, the AfD organised a conference called the 'Counter Summit' in Koblenz, Germany. This included Le Pen, the FPÖ's Harald Vilimsky, Wilders and Matteo Salvini (LN) and received a lot of media attention.[12] At the end of that year, in December 2017, ENF members including Le Pen and Wilders participated in an event in Prague at which they hailed the government coalition deal struck by the FPÖ as 'historic'.[13] Finally, Le Pen led a rally in Nice, France, in May 2018 'to celebrate recent gains on the continent and devise a battle plan for next year's European elections', in addition to launching a Europe-wide campaign against immigration. This event also featured Vilimsky, Wilders, Gerolf Annemans (VB) and Czech nationalist Tomio Okamura.[14]

While we have seen that the ENF parties do not make frequent use of their European affiliations in press releases, the various ENF leaders thus maintain a strong public picture of friendship and support. They celebrate each other's successes on social media and are regularly seen together in newspapers and on TV at official functions and private celebrations.[15] Geert Wilders, Marine Le Pen and Matteo Salvini are expert at taking group selfies and Le Pen, Salvini and Strache have even danced together.[16] These leaders have also courted publicity by holding bilateral meetings (e.g. Le Pen and Salvini in January 2016[17] and October 2018).[18] Finally, in an indication also of the degree to which the radical right is being mainstreamed in some Western media, Le Pen, Salvini, Strache and Wilders published a joint op-ed in the *Wall Street Journal* about how European civilisation and sovereignty are under threat from migrants.[19]

## *The stability of the ECR, EFDD, and ENF*

As Table 6.5 shows, there was a considerable amount of movement by individual MEPs in and out of the ECR, EFDD and ENF. However, only one party moved entirely from one group to another: the Sweden Democrats, which joined the ECR in July 2018. Otherwise, the main exits from the ECR, EFDD and ENF consisted of clusters of MEPs who split off from their party and found a home in one of the other two groups. This was the case for the AfD MEPs, Beatrix von Storch and Markus Pretzell, both of whom were part of the 'radical right' turn of that party (Decker 2016). In keeping with the fractious nature of the AfD, they belonged to different camps within its (now domestically dominant) radical right populist wing, and so they duly joined different EP groups, with von Storch moving to the EFDD and Pretzell to the ENF. Similarly, the fallout from the Front National's presidential election post-mortem in October 2017 saw the main proponent of the party's discredited 'Frexit' policy, Florian Philippot, and his ally Sophie Montel, move from the ENF to the EFDD (which housed several other FN exiles, too). The EFDD, unsurprisingly, is the group that saw most movement in and out. There was a steady trickle towards the exit of discontented Five Star, UKIP and individual MEPs, but the most significant departure given our focus in this book was the Sweden Democrats, which we shall discuss below.

Table 6.5: Party switches between groups, July 2014–January 2019

| From | To | ECR | EFDD | ENF | NI | Other groups |
|------|----|-----|------|-----|----|----|
| ECR   |    |   | 1 | 1 | – | – |
| EFDD  |    | 4 |   | 3 | 3 | 3 |
| ENF   |    | 1 | 4 |   | – | – |
| NI    |    | – | 3 | – |   | – |
| Others|    | 7 | – | – | – |   |

Notes: Excludes returning MEPs. Numbers denote number of MEPs that moved from one of the groups in the rows to a group in the column, e.g. seven MEPs from other groups joined the ECR.

The ECR announced on 3 July 2018 that it had accepted the two SD MEPs into the group.[20] While the leader of the UK Conservatives' EP delegation, Ashley Fox, told the media that his party had opposed the move since they felt it was too soon, he argued that the SD had nonetheless made significant progress 'in reforming themselves, expelling any members displaying unacceptable views or behaviour and diversifying their party base'.[21] In the past, Conservative opposition would likely have been enough to block the move, but following the 2016 Brexit referendum it was known that they would be leaving the group, and this appears to have diminished their power within the ECR.

The SD's move was no surprise to us. First, we already knew from our 2014 interviews that the party's ultimate goal was to sit alongside the Danish People's Party and that it prized the respectability that 'marrying up' in its European alliances could provide. Second, we were told by various interviewees in May 2017 that this switch was on the cards. As the senior UKIP official revealed to us in May 2017, unlike the Danish People's Party and Finns Party when they left UKIP's side in 2014, the Sweden Democrats had been 'completely upfront with us' and gave their partners plenty of warning over a year beforehand. The SD MEP Peter Lundgren had apparently informed UKIP that, although he was happy with them, 'I've been told from Stockholm that we have to go to the ECR'. It was said the SD wanted the move to occur before the Swedish general election in September 2018, to improve its chances of being accepted as a potential partner by the Moderates, Sweden's main centre-right party. As the leading SD MP, Richard Jomshof, explained to us in May 2017:

> Our image is very important because if we would be in the same group as the Conservatives in England, of course the Moderate party, I'm sure they could say, "But hey, they are with the Conservatives, and we all know that they are good. They're okay." So it will be easier for them [to accept us]. I think so.

While the Conservatives were important, however, Jomshof emphasised that his priority was 'to work together with the Finns and the Danish People's Party'. As we discussed in Chapter 3, the Danish People's Party (DF) and Finns Party (PS) had in 2014 ruled out cooperation with the SD. It is interesting, therefore, to see how their views evolved over subsequent years. In 2015, the DF MEP Anders Vistisen expressed doubts similar to those he had in the previous year concerning the SD, telling us that 'they are quite far away from being where they need to be'. In particular, he thought 'they need to show in Sweden that they can control their extreme element and stick to that for a number of years before there's any prospect for them getting in'. The MEP, and future leader of PS, Jussi Halla-aho was more amenable to the SD, telling us in 2015, 'Their future membership has not been ruled out. It has been stated that their reputation is not as good as it should be, but if they do their job properly during this term, then the question could be reconsidered'.

Two years later, in May 2017, both Vistisen and Halla-aho were far more open to the idea. Vistisen commented that the SD's decision in 2014 not to go with the ENF had enabled them to sustain the possibility of one day joining 'what we would define as the more acceptable Eurosceptic family'. He added, 'They have not disqualified themselves by going the Le Pen way'. In fact, and in contrast to his earlier positions, he told us that his party and the Finns would now support the SD joining the ECR. He explained that, as the word of an applicant's geographical neighbours holds more weight, their support would boost the SD's chances:

> I don't think we would block them. I don't think the Finns would block them either and the logic in these things is that normally the closest neighbours are the ones who are primarily estimating new parties, since that's the logical thing. I rely on my Croatian colleague if Slovenians are coming. I rely on my Latvian colleagues if Estonians were coming. Then they will probably rely on the Danes and Finns with the Swedes coming.

Two main reasons were given for this change in opinion. Firstly, Vistisen said that the SD had taken a stricter line with controversial and xenophobic figures in their party, something he believed they had demonstrated by expelling their entire youth wing for its extremist views in September 2015.[22] Secondly, size matters. In other words, the rise in popularity of the SD meant that it would likely increase the size of its delegation at the 2019 EP elections. As Vistisen acknowledged, 'If people who are, in these numbers, four to six mandates, are coming and asking to join, you reflect a little bit before you say "no", to be honest'. Halla-aho of the PS was similarly positive in May 2017 about the prospect of SD joining and explained to us the role that his party and the DF were playing in this process within the ECR. As he put it: 'We and the Danes have been active in this question and we have talked about it to the other small delegations and most of them seem to agree that there are no obstacles'. Like Vistisen, he also pointed to the SD's electoral rise as facilitating their inclusion, telling us:

> The situation is developing very rapidly in Sweden too. It's one thing to talk about affiliation or co-operation with a party whose support is 5 per cent, but now it seems very likely that they will be the largest or the second largest party in the next parliamentary elections in Sweden and that has a tendency to change perceptions.

A further contributing factor was the ideological development of the Finns Party itself, of which Halla-aho would be elected leader in June 2017, the month after we interviewed him. He explained that 'our party is becoming more radical in its positions' and, as a result, 'it will be easier for us to create alliances with parties like the Sweden Democrats'. So, while he acknowledged the problematic history of the SD as being very different from his own party (something which, as we saw in UK Conservative MEP Dan Hannan's comment in Chapter 3 about the SD having been 'really a racist party', was crucial in determining which parties were accepted into the ECR in 2014), Halla-aho argued that the parties were moving towards one another. Moreover, he indicated clearly that, as Finns Party leader, he would be less fearful than Timo Soini of adverse domestic media reactions. As Halla-aho explained:

> Our histories are different. We are a former rural, agrarian party and they have their neo-Nazi past. For us, or let's say for our party and its historical predecessor, migration issues were kind of a side issue, whereas for the Sweden Democrats, they have always been at the top of the agenda. But I believe we have moved towards that direction and, on the other hand, the Sweden Democrats has purged the questionable elements from the party during this decade. So, I believe we have drawn closer. It's clear that our current chairman doesn't feel comfortable with the Sweden Democrats, but I don't think that has so much to do with the substantial political questions. It's rather that he would have to answer difficult questions made by the media.

This acceptance from both the Danish People's Party and the Finns Party—the two parties which the Sweden Democrats had long wanted to sit alongside—marked an important milestone in the SD's journey from pariah to mainstream partner. While it has not yet achieved this status in Sweden, the party has surely moved closer to that goal by avoiding the ENF, joining the EFDD, and finally being accepted by the ECR. In that sense, the successive and increasingly respectable European marriages of the SD mean that its first term in the European Parliament was an unqualified success.

*Conclusion*

In this chapter, we have seen how, far from forming a 'right-wing Eurosceptic bloc' as some had feared, the three groups containing radical right populist parties displayed less internal cohesion in their voting behaviour than all other EP groups. Moreover, with the exception of the Danish People's Party, radical right populists continued to show little interest in participating in the work of the parliament. If they were not particularly united or active within parliament, their activities as groups outside it were not especially noteworthy either. The EP group 'brand'—be it ECR, EFDD or ENF—seems to have had little domestic recognition or value; in this sense, these EP group labels appear to have much less worth for radical right populists than the prospect of one day being able to say they were in the EPP did for Italy's Alleanza Nazionale in the 1990s. Nonetheless, we can see that being able to flaunt connections with individual leaders, past and present, from their EP partners does have value for radical right populists. In particular, the willingness of leaders such as Wilders, Le Pen and Salvini to be seen regularly together—and not just in serious discussions, but enjoying each other's company— is a new development and indicative of the 'proud populist' image which we discussed in Chapter 5. Finally, these groups were, by and large, reasonably stable, with the Sweden Democrats the only full party delegation to move from one group to another (this being entirely coherent with its view of the function of EP alliances). In the next, concluding, chapter, we will pick up some of these themes and consider what the future holds for radical right populists in the post-2019 EP.

7

# FROM INTERNATIONAL POPULISM TO TRANSNATIONAL POPULISM

We began this book by saying that radical right populism is on the rise internationally. We can begin the concluding chapter by saying that 'international radical right populism' is also on the rise. By this we mean that the international connections between radical right populists are increasing both in quantity and quality. Where once they shunned one another, most are now happy to parade their affinities and shared missions. These connections may be informal, like Nigel Farage speaking at a Donald Trump campaign rally or Matteo Salvini exchanging a series of friendly tweets with Jair Bolsonaro.[1] However, they can also be formal, as we have seen in this book, through alliances in the European Parliament. In the 2014–2019 EP, more radical right populists were in groups than ever before. These included, firstly, the 'proud populists' of the Front National, Vlaams Belang, Dutch Party for Freedom and Austrian Freedom Party, who had previously been isolated amongst the non-aligned but were able to sit happily together, with the Italian Lega Nord, in the ideologically homogenous ENF group. Secondly, they also included what we have termed the 'respectable radicals': the Danish People's Party, Finns Party and the Sweden Democrats, who preferred respectability over policy congruence and all, eventually, ended up together in the same ECR group as the UK Conservatives. In short, whether they pursued 'respectable radical' or 'proud populist' alliance strategies, western European radical right populists came of age in the 2014–2019 EP. None of them were alone in the Non-Inscrits and, with the exception of the Brexiting and imploding UKIP, all of them finished the legislature in a group with those other radical right populists they considered most like themselves.

We posed the question in the introductory chapter: why should we care about what parties do in the European Parliament? Certainly, some of the material from our interviews suggests that, beyond the MEPs in their Brussels/Strasbourg bubble, the parties themselves can hold ambivalent attitudes to this. And it is true that the group 'brand' does not matter to radical right populist parties in the same way as the EPP brand, for example, was once an important goal for Italy's Alleanza Nazionale in their domestic quest for respectability (see Chapter 2). This is unsurprising, given the 'oldest' of the three groups containing contemporary radical right populist parties in the 2014–2019 parliament, the ECR, only dated back to 2009, while the EFDD and ENF were completely new. There has therefore been little opportunity for RRP parties to build up, among their national publics, awareness of the EP groups they sit in. Moreover, we saw in Chapter 6 that representatives of the Danish People's Party acknowledged their voters and even their own grassroots members had little idea of which group they belonged to in the European Parliament. Indeed, even Jussi Halla-aho, MEP and current leader of the Finns Party, confessed to us that: 'When I became a member of the Finnish parliament in 2011, I have to admit, I didn't know which party we belonged to in the European Parliament. It only became clear to me gradually'.

Nonetheless, while the easily-forgotten group acronyms may have little purchase domestically, associations with specific foreign parties or politicians are highly prized. For the Danes and Finns, being able to be draw domestically on recognition of the mainstream Conservative Party from the UK and its historical figures, such as Churchill and Thatcher, was clearly perceived as important. But it was also important for a domestically marginalised party, like the Vlaams Belang, to be associated with major radical right populist parties in other countries. And the propensity of Salvini, Le Pen and Wilders for taking selfies with each other and posting them on social media suggests they also believe parading their union is good for their images.

Notwithstanding the lack of knowledge about EP groups, we have shown that there is much to be learned from how and why radical right populists do—and don't—co-operate with one another at the European level. It can tell us how these parties see themselves (as 'respectable radicals' or 'proud populists'), how other parties see them (as potential partners or pariahs) and how RRP parties are seeking to position themselves nationally and internationally. As radical right populists have moved from being minor to major parties in countries like Denmark, France, Italy and Sweden, they have also moved from the margins of the EP towards groups that reflect their self-images and goals—just as other ideological types have done for decades in the European Parliament. In his book on the far right, Cas Mudde (2019: forthcoming) argues that 'in the fourth wave, which roughly started in the twenty-first century, radical right parties have become mainstreamed and, increasingly, normalised, not just in Europe, but across the world'.[2] When we look at events in the EP, however, such development has not been uniform, as these parties must still choose between 'mainstreaming' like the Sweden Democrats (aspiring to membership of the ECR) and 'normalising' like the Lega Nord (by following policy congruence with the ENF).

To sum up, it is worth returning to the puzzle with which we began this study, five years ago. At the 2014 EP elections, the radical right populists of the Front

National, UKIP and the Danish People's Party all came first in their respective countries. And yet, in the 2014–2019 parliament, they sat in three different EP groups: Europe of Nations and Freedom (ENF), Europe of Freedom and Direct Democracy (EFDD) and European Conservatives and Reformists (ECR). So, why was there not a single radical right populist group? After all, we know that by far the main driver of EP alliances is policy congruence (McElroy and Benoit 2010, 2011; Bressanelli 2012; Maurer et al. 2008). Ideological birds of a feather flock together. That is why we find centre-right with centre-right, centre-left with centre-left, radical left with radical left, etc. Was it perhaps the case that, despite the common 'radical right populist' label which scholars have applied to these parties, they did not actually fit so neatly together in terms of policy positions? Using Chapel Hill Expert Survey data, as we have done in Chapters 3, 4, and 5, we can examine this for all the radical right populists considered in this book. Figure 7.1 maps their positions on their most important policy issues—immigration and Euroscepticism—as well as on the more general socio-economic and social left-right dimensions.

Figure 7.1 shows that our nine Western European RRP parties were highly congruent. All of them were clearly anti-immigration and strongly Eurosceptic. We see a similar fit on the social left–right dimension, meaning they generally agreed on issues like law and order and social conservatism. The only place we find greater

Figure 7.1: Positions of nine radical right populist parties in 2014

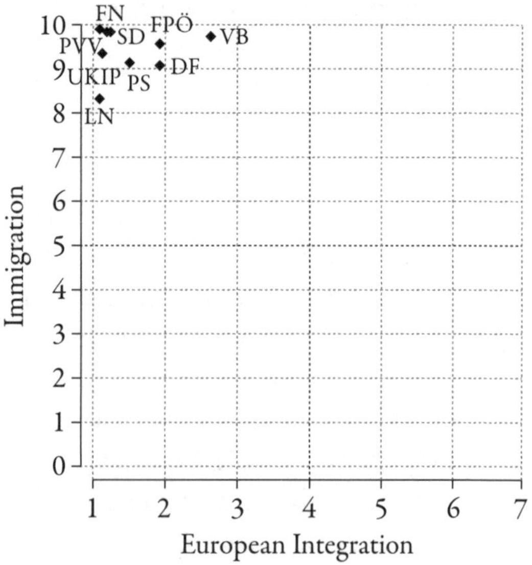
FN
FPÖ
VB
SD
PVV
DF
UKIP
PS
LN
10
9
8
7
6
5
4
3
2
1
0
Immigration
1
2
3
4
5
6
7
European Integration

Source: Own calculations based on Chapel Hill Expert Survey data 2014 (Bakker et al. 2015).

deviation is on the economic left–right dimension, where a few parties (especially UKIP and Vlaams Belang) have more right-wing, pro-deregulation positions, while other RRP parties are in the middle of this dimension. In general, though, the nine RRP parties that we have focused on in this book were highly congruent in their positions. Thus, policy congruence theory would predict that, once the radical right populist parties in the EP had the numbers to form a single common group, they would have done so.

To understand why they did not form a single EP group, which alliances they did form, and the logics driving these choices, we looked not only at why RRP parties joined their specific groups, but also at why they would not, or could not, ally with RRP parties in other groups. Building on the well-established framework of parties seeking policy, office or votes in the alliances they make (Müller and Strøm 1990), we found that each mechanism broadly underpins one of the three groups containing radical right populists in the 2014–2019 parliament. The ENF, including FN, PVV, FPÖ, VB and LN, was created as a coherent 'policy' group with the common mission of saving their nations and Europe from corrupt elites and dangerous 'others', notably immigrants (especially Muslims). This group represents what we might term a 'marriage of love' for these parties, since they finally embraced their commonalities, rooted in core policies of anti-immigration and Euroscepticism. Consistent with the shared ideology of its parties, we found that the ENF was inactive within the relatively low-profile EP decision-making process, but communicated its positions and unity through high-profile, widely-publicised events, usually featuring its leaders. The EFDD, on the other hand, followed mainly the logic of 'office', providing its constituent parties with the perks of group membership in terms of speaking time, financial resources and, if they were interested, with roles in the EP decision-making processes. Given this highly instrumental attitude to what they themselves described as a 'marriage of convenience', the EFDD parties—which included UKIP, M5S and for a long time also the Sweden Democrats—co-operated little either inside or outside the EP. Finally, the logic of the Danish People's Party, the Finns Party and later also the Sweden Democrats, to join the UK Conservative-led ECR was one of 'votes' (but also national office). The ECR was the most 'respectable marriage' they could aspire to in the EP. Their calculation was that by sitting alongside a highly regarded centre-right party like the UK Conservatives (and not alongside parties like the Front National, FPÖ, or even UKIP), they would create the impression at home, especially in the media, that they were now fully legitimised democratic parties and potential members of national government.

While the three groups followed these broad patterns, we identified other factors that shaped the necessary conditions for them to play out. In particular, leaders and histories were extremely important in determining which EP groups radical right populists could and did join. As we saw in Chapter 5, the ability of leaders like Le Pen, Salvini and Wilders to act with a freer hand than is the case for mainstream party leaders was crucial in enabling the ENF to form. In particular, Le Pen's capacity to change her party's image and strongly oppose her father as part of the FN's *dédiabolisation* was crucial to the creation of the ENF.

This leads us to the second factor: history. Multiple examples in our study point to the importance both of the history of RRP parties and how they are seen to deal with those in their parties who still cling to aspects of such histories. Parties like the Front National, the Austrian Freedom Party and the Sweden Democrats, with their extreme right, anti-Semitic or otherwise highly controversial pasts, were considered toxic (and unwilling to seriously address the reasons for this) by at least some other RRP parties. The Sweden Democrats are particularly interesting in this regard, as their alliance options in 2014 were shaped both by their fear of being tainted by association with old friends like the FN, but also by the UK Conservatives' and Danish People's Party's fears of being associated with them. And yet, as the journeys of the Sweden Democrats and the Front National show, radical right populists can overcome extremist histories and gain acceptance both from other RRPs with less controversial pasts, and even mainstream parties. Or, to use the metaphor we heard from interviewees across the parties, radical right populists can 'whitewash' their reputations, to some extent at least, by the alliances they make in the EP.

These reflections raise the question: what are the prospects for an eventual single radical right populist group in the EP? Can we envisage a situation in which the parties we have discussed in this book will all be able to form the type of lasting group found, for example, on the radical left? More generally, what might the future of radical right populist European co-operation look like? In the remainder of this conclusion, therefore, we will first consider the factors for and against a single EP group emerging in the coming years, then discuss why we think the future for these parties in Europe will increasingly involve not just international populism, but transnational populism.

## *Towards a single radical right populist group?*

On 8 April 2019, at a press conference in Milan, the MEP Anders Vistisen of the Danish People's Party (DF), Olli Kotro (2019 MEP candidate for the Finns Party), and Jörg Meuthen (MEP and lead candidate in the 2019 elections for the Alternative for Germany), appeared alongside the Lega Nord leader Matteo Salvini to announce that they would create a new group in the next parliament, provisionally called the European Alliance of Peoples and Nations (EAPN).[3] They signed a single-page document entitled *Towards a Common Sense Europe! Peoples Rise Up*, in which they pledged to 'establish a political group in the European Parliament after the elections with the aim to unite the patriotic and conservative forces in the European Parliament that are at the moment split over different groups'. Interestingly, the document explicitly stated that the parties were 'inspired by the idea of a Europe of co-operation' and were 'conscious of the need to reform the existing EU'. This would entail creating 'a safer Europe with well-protected external borders, less immigration and a stronger co-operation to tackle terrorism and Islamisation'.

Although there was some initial doubt about the exact composition of the proposed group, it became apparent that the EAPN would be a form of 'ENF Plus' when, the following month at a rally also in Milan, a large group of RRP leaders and party representatives shared the stage. Among these were Marine Le Pen, Geert Wilders and Salvini as well as Vistisen, Meuthen and the vice-chair of the Finns Party (PS) Laura Huhtasaari, along with MPs and leaders from Central and Eastern European parties that were not yet in the EP such as the Eesti Konservatiivne Rahvaerakond (EKRE—Conservative People's Party of Estonia), Slovakia's Sme Rodina (We are Family), Bulgaria's Volya (Will) and the Czech Svoboda a Prímá Demokracie (SPD—Freedom and Direct Democracy).[4] Of the radical right populist parties we have discussed in this book, only the Sweden Democrats declined to participate, as did their ECR partner, the Polish Law and Justice (PiS). After the 2019 elections, the EAPN became the 'Identity and Democracy' (ID) group, encompassing the ENF parties (apart from the PVV which did not win any seats), along with the AFD, DF, PS, EKRE and SPD.

The presence of the Danish People's Party and Finns Party in such company seemed very surprising given their 'respectable radicals' strategy during the 2014–2019 parliament. After all, these two parties had joined the ECR with the specific goals of improving their domestic image by sitting alongside the UK Conservatives and not having anything to do with parties like the Front National or even UKIP. As Vistisen of the Danish People's Party said to us in 2014, most other radical right populist parties 'would primarily give us problems or not do anything for us at all' and 'some of these parties have had a history that, in our perspective, you cannot come back from'. While his party had already changed its mind about the Sweden Democrats between 2014 and 2017 (see Chapter 6), it was nonetheless striking to find him, five years later, representing the DF on a stage in Milan with precisely those other parties.

Such apparent contradictions notwithstanding, there were a number of factors favouring the move of the Danish People's Party and Finns Party from the ECR towards this larger, but still ideologically homogenous, version of the ENF. The first is the presumed eventual departure, thanks to Brexit, of the UK Conservatives. As we saw in Chapters 3 and 6, being alongside the UK Conservatives in 2014 was considered by the DF and PS to be a source of pride and a signal to their domestic medias, elites and publics that they were fully legitimate parties and to be taken seriously. With the UK Conservatives on their way out, however, the 'respectability' dividend of not following policy congruence was reduced. Certainly, proclaiming to domestic audiences that they were in a group led by the Polish Law and Justice, which since 2014 has itself developed into a fully radical right populist party (and quite a controversial one, too), would not offer them the same type of respectability-by-association. Meanwhile, the parties of the ENF had become more respectable by 2019. Notably, both the Austrian FPÖ and the Lega Nord in Italy had once again taken seats in national cabinets during the 2014–2019 EP. Indeed, even a few months before that happened in Austria, Vistisen told us in May 2017 that, despite what he had said about the FPÖ's toxic past in 2014:

> You can say FPÖ is so mainstream in Austria now. When you can have almost half the vote in a presidential election, it is increasingly difficult for the rest of us to keep claiming that they are not, you know, an acceptable part of the political situation in Austria.

A second factor pushing the DF and PS to move was that, irrespective of reputational benefits or drawbacks, the prospect of being in an ECR which would soon have PiS as the only large party was not appealing. As Morten Messerschmidt of the Danish People's Party told us in March 2018, without the UK Conservatives in the ECR, 'we'd get entirely dominated by the Poles, which is a not very attractive thought, to have such a massive—

they might be even bigger next time—massive delegation'. Likewise, Jussi Halla-aho of the Finns Party said in our interview in May 2017: 'The main question is the balance of power in the new ECR. Most of us are concerned about the Poles and we would like to avoid a situation where they dominate very strongly this group and its image'.

Moreover, from our interviews we could see clearly that, while parties like the DF, PS and SD gave firm and often very pragmatic reasons why they could not sit with the likes of the FN or FPÖ, that is not to say that the idea appalled them. As we noted above, Vistisen of the DF recognised how excluding the FPÖ *a priori* was more problematic in 2017 than just a few years previously. In our interview with him in 2017, Halla-aho expressed this view more strongly, saying that he hoped for an alliance at some point in the future 'with certain other parties which are currently in the ENF, especially the Austrian party'. He continued: 'I'm very dissatisfied with the current situation where many parties that share very much are dispersed in three different groups' and concluded therefore that 'it would be desirable to have one large Eurosceptic, immigration critical group in the parliament'.

Interviewees from the ENF parties have expressed similar views since we first spoke to them in 2014 about the importance of radical right populists standing together, given the urgency of the issues they campaign on. When discussing those radical right populists like the Danish People's Party and the Sweden Democrats that had preferred to join the ECR and EFDD, De Danne (FN) claimed in our 2014 interview with him that, in five years or so, these parties would have to re-evaluate their 'respectable radicals' strategy. In his view:

> They will have to make a choice about the future of the European Union and what is going on about massive immigration, about globalism and so on. So, there is a moment they will not have the choice and the luxury to stay politically correct and to use the excuse of demonisation to the liberal media for example as an excuse not to join forces with us.

ENF interviewees were also very clear that it was not policy differences separating them from the radical right populists in the ECR and EFDD. As Johannes Hübner, an FPÖ MP responsible for the party's European and foreign policy, said to us in 2014: 'Most of the differences, they are fabricated'. He added that: 'If all the members and the party leaders would sit down, relax, listen to what they really think and feel about, they would find out that, actually this is a group of friends that understand [each other] quite well and they could co-operate quite well'.

However, it was not just the role of party history and the fear of domestic backlash that drove some radical right populist parties away from alliance with others. Another strong dividing issue between the radical right populists in the ECR and those in the ENF during the

2014–2019 parliament was their divergent positions on Russia and Vladimir Putin. The ENF parties have tended to be very supportive of Russia in recent years, viewing it as a natural ally. As the FN's De Danne explained to us in 2014: 'We are clear. We do not want a Europe which goes from Washington to Brussels. We want a Europe that goes from Lisbon to Vladivostok. So that means we want to be friends with a real European country, which is Russia'.

Others from his party and its ENF allies have gone further. For example, the FN's vice-president Louis Aliot (also Marine Le Pen's partner) has said that Putin's Russia is 'one of the last European defenders of the Judeo-Christian values that form the basis of our civilisation', while Salvini has praised Putin as 'a statesman who does not serve the interests of the globalists' (cited in Shekhovtsov 2017: 89–90). The links between these parties and Russia do not end with expressions of admiration. It was widely reported that Le Pen's party received a €9 million loan in 2014 from the First Czech Russia Bank, which some journalists claimed was approved by the Kremlin.[5] Similarly, in February 2019, the Italian news magazine *L'Espresso* published details of an alleged plan for people close to Putin to finance the Lega Nord's EP campaign to the tune of around €3 million.[6] Already in 2016, the leader of the FPÖ, Heinz-Christian Strache, signed a five-year co-operation agreement with Putin's party United Russia, which included plans for regular meetings and collaboration in various policy areas, amongst them migration.[7] However, this engagement with Russia proved to be the downfall of Strache, possibly with far-reaching damage for the FPÖ, when a video appeared in May 2019 that showed him and another senior FPÖ representative discussing the exchange of economic and political favours with an alleged Russian investor.[8]

The relationship of the major ENF parties with Russia appeared to be a red line for those we spoke to in the ECR during the 2014–19 Parliament. As the PiS MEP, Ryszard Czarnecki told us in May 2017, they had problems with 'very pro-Russian parties' like the FPÖ. The same month, Jomshof of the SD said in our interview: 'I don't understand why the National Front is so much into Russia or Putin. I mean, I don't understand it'. Similarly—and not surprisingly, given the history between Finland and Russia—Halla-aho told us in 2017 that the biggest single impediment stopping his party contemplating co-operation with Front National in the future was its 'peculiarly fond' attitude towards Putin and Russia.

So, what changed the minds of the Danes and the Finns in 2019 and led them to move together again to a new group, just as they had in 2014? With regards to the Russian issue, evidently they have weighed the domestic costs up and decided that either they are not as heavy as they thought, and/or that the benefits of being with like-minded radical right populist parties on the rise are worth any disadvantages. Just like other parties from the same ideological family that ally in the EP, they may have concluded that what unites them is much more substantial and important than what divides them.

Two factors, which we have already identified as crucial in radical right populist group formation, are also likely to be influential here: party leadership and domestic vote implications. Regarding the first, the Finns Party underwent a leadership change in June 2017 when the more radical Halla-aho took over and the moderate wing, led by defeated leadership candidate Sampo Terho, left to form a new party, 'Blue Reform'. As we have seen, Halla-aho believed that Eurosceptic, immigration-critical parties, as he described them, should not be divided in the EP and the Finns Party move is consistent with this. Moreover, we know that RRP leaders can usually force through changes in strategy and policy quickly and more easily than leaders of other parties. Thus, it seems likely that Halla-aho has driven the decision to move the PS in 2019.

The Danes, on the other hand, may have calculated that they do not need an international 'reputational shield' any more within domestic politics. The party has provided parliamentary support for the Danish centre-right in exchange for policy concessions on several occasions since 2001 and has also built better relations with the Social Democrats, to the extent that the DF envisages a potential future as a pivot party which can choose between the two main blocks. They seem to have reached their goal of sufficiently mainstreaming their image to be taken seriously by the Danish elites. On the other hand, this mainstreaming may have had the unintended consequence of opening up space for two new Danish parties on the right that were not present in 2014: Stram Kurs (Hard Line) and Nye Borgerlige (New Right). While these did not initially seem to pose a significant threat to the DF, the party declined by several percentage points in polls in the first half of 2019, with 16 per cent of those who voted for the DF in 2015 saying they would vote for one of the new radical right parties in 2019.[9]

We can therefore see a significant consolidation among radical right populists in the Identity and Democracy group. Nonetheless, even if/when the UK Conservatives leave the EP after Brexit, the ECR should continue, since PiS and the Sweden Democrats have said they will not join the Identity and Democracy group. For PiS, the issue of Russia simply remains too divisive and domestically damaging. For the Sweden Democrats, as one of its leading figures, Mattias Karlsson, said in a Facebook post after the DF and PS announced they were joining the EAPN (later ID), 'the future is not to isolate itself [sic] in a purely nationalist group with more or less radical and Putin-friendly parties'. Although Karlsson emphasised that the SD would continue to collaborate with them in the Nordic Council, he added that he regretted 'the signal about positioning from our sister parties'. Given what we have learned about the journey of the SD in this book, it is interesting to observe that, as of May 2019, the party intends to pursue a more moderate path at European level than those other Nordic populist parties it previously took as models for its own 'respectable radicals' strategy. It is also worth noting that there are new radical right populist parties like the Dutch Forum voor Democratie (FvD—Forum for Democracy) and Spain's Vox, that prefer the ECR.[10] In short, in the coming years we expect there to be one large ideologically homogenous radical right populist group, Identity and Democracy, but also an ECR that is smaller and more ideologically heterogenous, but also significantly more radical right populist, than it was in 2014.

Finally, it remains to be seen whether the Hungarian government party Fidesz will complete the journey towards being a fully-fledged member of Europe's radical right populist family, and if its fellow Hungarians from Jobbik will one day be accepted by other radical right populists as a legitimate EP partner. In recent years, Fidesz leader Viktor Orbán has held high-profile meetings with radical right populist leaders from other EU countries, in particular Jaroslaw Kaczynski of PiS and Salvini of the Lega Nord (who in turn met one another in January 2019).[11] Similar messages have come out of all these meetings. Kaczynski and Orbán talked about waging a 'cultural counter-revolution' to reform the EU, Orbán and Salvini spoke of 'walking down the same path' to oppose migration and the policies of French President Macron, and Kaczynski and Salvini discussed 'the future of Europe and how to give a new sense to the European dream'.[12] Such statements, and the fact that Orbán was threatened with expulsion from the Christian Democratic group EPP, point to the possibility of a group move by Fidesz. On the other hand, given Orbán's attempts to dismantle Hungarian liberal democracy, membership of the highly-respectable EPP continues to provide a valuable 'reputational shield' and Orbán is thus the ultimate 'respectable radical'. Certainly, if Fidesz did have to find a new home in the EP, we would expect it to be to alongside PiS in the ECR, given not only its warm relations with the former but also Orbán's comment in a May 2019 media interview that 'I have nothing at all to do with Madame Le Pen. Nothing'.[13]

Thus, domestic calculations as well as the size and composition of the radical right populist parties in the new EP will play an important role in the decisions around new group formations. Several factors seem to speak against one large group, among them the importance of 'reputational shields' to some parties, as well as highly salient issues like the relationship with Russia. At the same time, we may well see more inter-group cooperation than was the case in the 2014–2019 parliament. For example, Kaczynski, Salvini and Orbán have talked after their meetings of the need for co-operation on issues like 'growth, security, family and the Christian roots of Europe'. So, while they may continue to sit in different parts of the choir, they are increasingly in open agreement about the choice of hymns. Such declarations also speak to the fact that, as we discuss in the next section, radical right populists are increasingly presenting themselves not just as the saviours of their nations, but of Europe itself.

## *The Saviours of Europe*

While the prospects for a lasting, single, ideologically homogenous EP group containing all the main radical right populists in Europe remain uncertain, what we do believe will continue in the coming years is the growth both of international populism and of transnational populism (Moffitt 2017; De Cleen 2017). This means in practice that radical right populists present themselves not only as working with like-minded parties in EP groups in order to defend their national 'peoples' from a series of bad elites and 'dangerous others' threatening them at national level, but also as doing so to defend a European 'people' from elites and 'dangerous others' at continental level. As De Cleen (2017: 356) argues, contemporary radical right populists in Europe:

...have constructed an antagonism between ordinary people who resist multiculturalism and cherish their national identity, and national and European elites that are undermining national identity through lenient integration and migration policies. Especially when these parties actually co-operate on a European level, and certainly when their European political representatives speak for the entire political group (and thus for all the nations and people-as-underdogs the group claims to represent) a claim towards the representation of a transnational people-as-underdog is made.

We have argued in Chapter 5 that the ENF combined 'international populism' with 'transnational populism' and there are several reasons why we expect to see this mixture become more prominent for radical right populists. First, the simultaneous increase of (a) support for EU membership among national publics and (b) the electoral strength of many radical right populist parties means that it is both in their interests and more plausible for them to propose to remake Europe in their image rather than advocate exit (or simply refuse to engage). Second, the longstanding key issue for radical right populists—immigration—is now perceived by citizens across the continent as a pressing European issue even more than a national one. It therefore makes sense for RRPs to be seen to be active, together, at European level to tackle this. Third, radical right populists increasingly see themselves as part of a European and even a global political wave, rather than simply acting alone on national stages. And, as we have argued in this book, many are less fearful than in the past of co-operating with one another. Let us discuss these three factors in turn.

One of the most significant policy developments on the continental radical right in recent years has been the retreat from advocating EU exit for their countries or from positions that are tantamount to this. Rather, as the meetings between Salvini, Orbán and Kaczynski mentioned earlier indicate, they are now seeking to reform the EU in line with their common worldviews. In part, this reflects the fact that support for leaving the EU has declined across the Union since the UK voted for Brexit in June 2016. For example, despite the Eurosceptic governing coalition of M5S and Lega Nord enjoying strong public support, 65 per cent of Italians in December 2018 wanted to remain in the EU (and 64 per cent wished also to stay in the Euro).[14] Likewise, in Austria, where the FPÖ had been in government alongside the centre-right since 2017, 74 per cent of respondents in October 2018 said they did not think the country should leave the EU.[15] In Denmark, where the Danish People's Party had been pushing for a referendum and Eurosceptic attitudes have traditionally been strong, survey results published at the beginning of 2019 showed that support for remaining in the EU was at its highest level in decades, with 62 per cent saying they did not want a referendum on EU membership and 66 per cent saying they would vote to remain if such a referendum were held (with just 22 per cent stating they would vote to leave).[16] Very similar results were reported in Sweden in June 2018, with 66 per cent saying they wanted the country to remain in the EU and 23 per cent saying they preferred to leave.[17]

Radical right populists have reacted to these public shifts. For example, in an op-ed for one of the main Swedish newspapers, *Aftonbladet*, on 31 January 2019, Sweden Democrats leader Jimmie Åkesson announced that his party would seek to change the EU from within, alongside its European allies, rather than fight for a referendum and leave.[18] We have seen analogous moves by the Front National (now Rassemblement National) since the 2017 Presidential election, and the Lega Nord since the 2018 Italian general election. Having first played down the salience of its Eurosceptic positions in the weeks between the first and second rounds, the FN retreated after the 2017 election from its opposition both to French EU membership and participation in the Euro. Meanwhile, in Italy, Salvini has made it clear that his party wishes to reform the EU and no longer prioritises a 'Euro exit' policy.[19] On the contrary, as he put it in January 2019, he wants to 'save Europe'.[20]

And why would radical right populists want to leave the EU now anyway? They are no longer minor parties that have no hope of sitting at the Union's decision table. Take Salvini, who, before the 2014 EP election was touring Italy on his 'Basta Euro' ('Enough of the Euro') tour.

At the time, he led a party that had received just 4 per cent of the vote in the 2013 general election. Five years later, in the run-up to the 2019 EP election, his party was in government and hovering around 33 per cent in opinion polls, over ten percentage points ahead of its closest rival and coalition partner, the M5S. Being part of the national government, of course, has also given the Lega a presence in the Council of the European Union since 2018, alongside parties like FPÖ, Fidesz, PiS and, most recently, EKRE. And, even where they cannot access national government, radical right populist parties are doing better than ever. The Sweden Democrats received their highest share of the vote to date at the 2018 general election and are hot on the heels of the two major parties. The previous year, Marine Le Pen secured a third of the vote in the second round of the presidential election and it was considered a disappointment, as she had harboured hopes of winning. In short, radical right populists are reaching a point where their combined forces at European level, whether in parliament or intergovernmental institutions like the Council of Ministers, could give them a strong voice. As Chryssogelos (2019) has argued, 'The political stage on which they perform today is transnational, and this allows them to pursue in tandem the dual goal of dominating their countries' domestic politics and increasing their influence in EU proceedings'. Or, as Philippe Olivier, a senior advisor (and brother-in-law) to Marine Le Pen, told us in

October 2018, the rise of similar parties to his across Europe means that, within the EU institutions, 'We might have either a blocking minority or a majority to change things from the inside'. Given that favourable situation, he added, 'it would be ridiculous to leave'.

The second reason why we expect to see not just more international populism, but also transnational populism, is that the key issues for RRPs (first and foremost immigration, but also the linked question of terrorism) are perceived by voters as being most pressing at European level. This has become much more salient during and after the 2015 refugee crisis. However, it might have been a double-edged sword for the radical right populist parties. On one hand, it increased the potential for conflict between these parties because of discussions regarding the distribution of refugees. While parties like the Italian Lega Nord appealed to the common European responsibility, many other radical right populist—and thus nativist—parties refused to let refugees into their countries. On the other hand, the crisis has made immigration the key transnational issue; we can see this quite clearly if we look at recent Eurobarometer results from the countries of the eight ECR, EFDD and ENF parties we have focused on in this book (excluding the UK given its lesser future relevance). Tables 7.1 and 7.2 allow us to compare the most important issues according to citizens of the eight countries since the run-up to the last EP elections in 2014. While immigration has been con-

Table 7.1: The two most important issues facing our country

|  | 2014 | 2015 | 2016 | 2017 | 2018 |
|---|---|---|---|---|---|
| Austria | Unemploy. Govt. debt | Unemploy. Immigration | Immigration Unemploy. | Immigration Unemploy. | Immigration Ht/soc sec. |
| Belgium | Unemploy. Ec. Situation | Unemploy. Immigration | Terrorism Immigration | Terror+Immi Unemploy. | Immigration Pensions |
| Denmark | Unemploy. Ht/soc sec. | Immigration Ht/soc sec. | Immigration Ht/soc sec. | Immigration H/s+environm | H/s+Immi Enviro |
| Finland | Unemploy. Ec. Situation | Unemploy. Ec. Situation | Unemploy. Ec. Situation | Ht/soc sec. Unemploy. | Ht/soc sec. Unemploy. |
| France | Unemploy. Ec. Situation | Unemploy. Ec. Situation | Unemploy. Terrorism | Unemploy. Terrorism | Unemploy. Terrorism |
| Italy | Unemploy. Ec. Situation | Unemploy. Immigration | Unemploy. Ec. Situation | Unemploy. Immigration | Unemploy. Immigration |

*Table continued*

| | | | | | |
|---|---|---|---|---|---|
| Netherlands | Unemploy. Ht/soc sec. | Ht/soc sec. Unemploy. | Immigration Ht/soc sec. | Ht/soc sec. Immigration | Ht/soc sec. Enviro |
| Sweden | Unemploy. Education | Unemploy. Education | Immigration H/s+Educ. | Ht/soc sec. Immigration | Ht/soc sec. Education |

Note: For each year, we have taken the May edition of Eurobarometer, with the exception of 2018 (March). Given space restrictions, we use a number of abbreviations: 'Ht/soc sec' = 'health and social security'; 'Unemploy.' = 'unemployment', 'Enviro' = 'environment, climate and energy issues'. When a '+' is used, it means that both categories got the same percentage.

Source: http://ec.europa.eu/commfrontoffice/publicopinion/index.cfm

Table 7.2: The two most important issues facing the EU

| | 2014 | 2015 | 2016 | 2017 | 2018 |
|---|---|---|---|---|---|
| Austria | Mem. Fin. / Unemploy. | Immigration / Mem. Fin. | Immigration / Terrorism | Immigration / Terrorism | Immigration / Mem. Fin. |
| Belgium | Ec. Situation / Unemploy. | Immigration / Unemploy. | Immigration / Terrorism | Terrorism / Immigration | Immigration / Terrorism |
| Denmark | Ec.Sit+Unemploy. / Immigration | Immigration / Ec. Situation | Immigration / Terrorism | Immigration / Terrorism | Immigration / Terrorism |
| Finland | Ec. Situation / Mem. Fin. | Mem. Fin. / Ec. Situation | Immigration / Terrorism | Terrorism / Immigration | Immigration / Terrorism |
| France | Ec. Situation / Unemploy. | Immigration / Ec. Situation | Terrorism / Immigration | Terrorism / Immigration | Immigration / Terrorism |
| Italy | Unemploy. / Ec. Situation | Immigration / Unemploy. | Immigration / Terrorism | Terrorism / Immigration | Immigration / Unemploy. |

*Table continued*

| | | | | | |
|---|---|---|---|---|---|
| Netherlands | Ec. Situation Unemploy. | Immigration Mem. Fin. | Immigration Terrorism | Immigration Terrorism | Immigration Mem. Fin. |
| Sweden | Ec. Situation Unemploy. | Immigration Ec. Situation | Immigration Terrorism | Immigration Clim. Change | Immigration Clim. Change |

Note: As in the previous table, for each year, we have taken the May edition of Eurobarometer, with the exception of 2018 (March). In addition to the abbreviations explained in the previous note, here we also use 'Mem. Fin.' for 'the state of member states' public finances'.

Source: http://ec.europa.eu/commfrontoffice/publicopinion/index.cfm

sistently listed as the most important one facing Austria and Denmark since the 2015 refugee crisis and has often been cited as the second most important in Italy, it is constantly either the first or second most important issue facing the EU right across our cases. Moreover, since the refugee crisis, either immigration, or the closely related issue of terrorism (given that RRPs link the two), has been deemed the most pressing concern facing the EU in all eight countries. This reached a peak in the Spring 2018 Eurobarometer, when immigration was considered the single most important issue facing the EU in all eight countries.

These results underline the current importance of the European level for radical right populists. They have publicly salient issues that unite them and which are perceived as being first and foremost challenges facing the EU. As Thierry Mariani, a former centre-right Minister in the Nicolas Sarkozy government who moved party to become the lead candidate for Rassemblement National (the former FN) in the 2019 EP election, said to us in November 2018: 'What unites people in the EPP from France, Lithuania and Poland? Not much. By contrast, we have two or three subjects that unite us. First of all, a question of identity. It's the triptych of identity-migration-religion. Because, in reality, with identity, we're talking about Islam and immigration.'[21]

Radical right populists are thus able today to cast themselves not only as the saviours of their respective national 'peoples' against bad elites and 'others' who wish to undermine the people's sovereignty, identity and well-being, but also as the saviours of a European people from the dangers posed by secular elites in national capitals and Brussels, and 'others', especially Muslims, who are said to pose a continent-wide threat. Their 'people' is not merely national, but transnational. Consistent with this, Marine Le Pen, Geert Wilders and Matteo Salvini are not just prominent national political figures, but international ones. Indeed, they are perhaps more international than many mainstream party leaders in their respective countries. For example, Dittrich (2017: 9) found that 40 per cent of Marine Le Pen's Facebook 'likes' came from abroad, as opposed to 35 per cent for Emanuel Macron. Similarly, Froio and Ganesh (2018: 20) note that Le Pen 'enjoys a genuinely transnational audience on Twitter'. The same is true of Geert Wilders, who began developing a global populist profile many years ago, speaking abroad not only in European countries such as Britain, but also in Australia and the United States, about the dangers Christian people across the West were facing from a surreptitious and global drive for 'Islamisation'.[22]

This brings us to our final point. Radical right populists in Europe today do not feel they are alone. As we have seen, 'respectable radicals' strategies notwithstanding, the 2014–2019 European parliament was the first in which all Western European radical right populists finished the legislature alongside those other RRPs that they considered most similar to them. They are parties that are increasingly unashamed of their commonalities and proudly parade them. Moreover, they see their influence rising not just at national level, but at European level and beyond. As Le Pen's advisor, Philippe Olivier, said to us in October 2018: 'This is a global movement. Trump did not happen by accident. Brexit did not happen by accident. Modi in India did not happen by accident. Putin did not happen by accident'. The rise of international and transnational populism in Europe has not happened by accident either. The EU has created the stage to bring these parties together at European level. And now, they are finally stepping onto it.

# APPENDIX

## LIST OF INTERVIEWEES

| | *Name* | *Party* | *Dates* | *Role at time of interview* |
|---|---|---|---|---|
| 1. | Gerolf Annemans | VB | July 2014 & June 2015 | MEP; former party leader |
| 2. | Nicolas Bay | FN | July 2014 | MEP, close to Marine Le Pen |
| 3. | David Borrelli | M5S | July 2014 | MEP; co-chair EFDD |
| 4. | Aymeric Chauprade | FN | June 2015 | MEP; responsible for FN foreign relations |
| 5. | Ignazio Corrao | M5S | June 2015 | MEP |
| 6. | Ryszard Czarnecki | PiS | May 2017 | MEP & EP vice-president |
| 7. | Ludovic De Danne | FN | July 2014 | EU/EP advisor to Marine Le Pen |
| 8. | Kent Ekeroth | SD | June 2014 | SD International Secretary |
| 9. | Lorenzo Fontana | LN | June 2015 | MEP; very close to Salvini |

| | | | |
|---|---|---|---|
| 10. Jussi Halla-Aho | PS | June 2015 & May 2017 | MEP (subsequently party leader) |
| 11. Daniel Hannan | Con | July 2014 | MEP |
| 12. Lucas Hartong | PVV | June 2015 | Former MEP (2010–14) |
| 13. Roger Helmer | UKIP | July 2014 | MEP |
| 14. Hans-Olaf Henkel | AfD | June 2015 | MEP |
| 15. Johannes Hübner | FPÖ | July 2014 | MP, responsible for European & Foreign policy |
| 16. Richard Jomshof | SD | June 2014 & May 2017 | MP (considered one of three or four main figures in SD) |
| 17. Karsten Lorentzen | DF | March 2018 | Foreign policy advisor. Former EP official for DF, 2009–14. |
| 18. Petr Mach | SSO | June 2015 | MEP & party leader |
| 19. Thierry Mariani | FN/RN | November 2018 | Former Minister in Sarkozy government. Moved to FN/RN in January 2019. |
| 20. Morten Messerschmidt | DF | March 2018 | MEP |
| 21. Andreas Mölzer | FPÖ | August 2014 | Former MEP (2004–14) |

## APPENDIX

| | | | |
|---|---|---|---|
| 22. Philippe Olivier | FN/RN | October 2018 | Leading advisor to Marine Le Pen |
| 23. Fiorello Provera | LN | July 2014 | Former MEP (2009–14) |
| 24. Francesco Speroni | LN | July 2014 | Former MEP (1999–2014) |
| 25. Sampo Terho | PS | July 2014 | MEP |
| 26. Gawain Towler | UKIP | October 2018 | Former UKIP & EFD Press officer |
| 27. Geoffrey Van Orden | Con | June 2015 | MEP; vice-chair of ECR group |
| 28. Tom Van Grieken | VB | June 2015 | Party leader |
| 29. Anders Vistisen | DF | July 2014, June 2015 & May 2017 | MEP |
| 30. FPÖ official | FPÖ | July 2014 | Leading party advisor on EU/EP |
| 31. UKIP official | UKIP | July 2014, June 2015 & May 2017 | Leading EU-level advisor to UKIP and EFDD |

# NOTES

## 1. INTERNATIONAL POPULISM

1. While Front National became Rassemblement National (National Rally) in June 2018 and the Italian Lega Nord has been known since 2017 simply as 'La Lega' (The League), for the sake of consistency, in this book we generally use their names as they were at the time of the 2014 EP elections.
2. As demonstrated by the rise of the Sweden Democrats since 2010, the Alternative for Germany since 2014 and, since 2018, Vox in Spain.
3. See: https://www.bbc.com/news/world-europe-24924372
4. Many newspapers including *The Guardian*, *The Economist*, *The Financial Times* and *The New York Times*, ran numerous pieces on the prospects for radical right populists at the European level in the year before the EP election. See, for example: Jan-Werner Müller (2013) 'How Europe could face its own shutdown', https://www.theguardian.com/commentisfree/2013/oct/21/europe-own-shutdown-anti-eu-parties; *The Economist* (2013) 'The anti-European question', https://www.economist.com/news/2013/11/18/the-anti-european-question; Tony Barber (2014) 'Predictions of populist takeover in Europe are far fetched',

https://www.ft.com/content/4fd0f5f4-db57-11e3-b112-00144feabdc0

5. We count MEPs from all the parties in Table 1.1, along with three from Jobbik.

6. We did try in 2015 to interview MEPs from Jobbik, to discuss their exclusion by other radical right populist parties. The only reply we received was from Krisztina Morvai's office, who told us that 'as a matter of policy Ms. Morvai does not give any interviews to foreign press and universities'. Not being able to acquire Hungarian citizenship, we had no way of meeting this unusually strict and specific condition.

7. See, for example, Minkenberg (2017) who considers Fidesz 'right-wing populist', but not 'radical right'. For an alternative view, see Mudde (2019) who argues that Fidesz has fully transformed while in government into a radical right populist party.

8. See: http://www.europarl.europa.eu/elections2014-results/en/turnout.html. It is worth noting that, as in previous years, there was considerable variation in turnouts across the EU in the 2014 EP elections, ranging from 13 and 18 per cent in Slovakia and the Czech Republic, to over 80 per cent in Belgium and Luxembourg.

9. You will have to read the whole book to find out who this is.

10. At the 2018 Swedish general election, the Sweden Democrats finished third with 17.5 per cent, behind the centre-right Moderate Party on 19.8 per cent, and the Social Democrats on 28.3 per cent.

## 2. RADICAL RIGHT POPULISTS AND GROUP FORMATION IN THE EUROPEAN PARLIAMENT

1. In previous decades, some of the parties we focus on were actually in favour of greater integration (e.g. FN in the mid-1980s and LN for most of the 1990s).
2. For example, Kitschelt and McGann (1995: 201) had argued 'it is questionable, however, whether the negative electoral coalition brought together by populist parties will stick together once these parties have to act on policy problems as governing parties'. Similarly, Mény and Surel (2002: 18) asserted that populists were 'by nature neither durable nor sustainable parties of government'.
3. While we view Podemos as a borderline case of populism in 2019, we follow the (current and continuing) convention among scholars to include it among left-wing populist parties (e.g. Rooduijn et al. 2019).
4. See, for example, the tensions in late 2018 around the Austrian proposal to give citizenship to German-speaking residents of the region: https://www.bbc.com/news/world-europe-45888287
5. See: https://www.theguardian.com/world/2007/nov/15/eu.thefarright
6. AN was refused entry into the EPP, although its (former) representatives eventually became EPP MEPs, thanks to AN's fusion in 2008 with Silvio Berlusconi's Forza Italia to create the Popolo della Libertà (PdL—People of Freedom). The PdL continued Forza Italia's membership of the EPP.
7. These issues notwithstanding, we cross-checked our results from the CHES data for Euroscepticism and immigration with the data from the Euromanifesto project (EES 2015;

Schmitt et al. 2018). Although the Euromanifesto data finds substantially more variation between the eventual ENF parties than the CHES data, there is no general trend towards more coherence over time, which is in line with our findings. As a further robustness check, we also compared the CHES data from 2014 with the party positions from the euandi (pronounced 'EU and I') survey. While primarily a voting advice application for voters, euandi collected party positions in the run-up to the 2014 EP elections by asking groups of country experts to place parties on policy dimensions similar to those of CHES. These experts were asked to base their scores on party documents. Additionally, the parties were asked both to place themselves and to evaluate their placements by the country experts (Garzia et al. 2017). We find that the positions of CHES and euandi match well, especially on the EU integration and the immigration dimension.
8. http://www.europarl.europa.eu/meps/en/home
9. http://www.europarl.europa.eu/groups/accounts_en.htm
10. See, for example, https://www.ft.com/content/aad578e8-e463-11e3-a73a-00144feabdc0

## 3. EUROPEAN CONSERVATIVES AND REFORMISTS: A VERY RESPECTABLE MARRIAGE

1. See the original document, cited in full in the appendix of Bale at al 2010.
2. As Bale et al. (2010) discuss in their article, sitting alongside PiS and ODS had already generated criticism of the Conservatives in the British media.
3. Our ECR interviewees were as follows. Danish People's

Party (3): two MEPs (one of whom we interviewed three times, in 2014, 2015 and 2017) and one senior advisor/official; Finns Party (2): two MEPs (one of whom, the current leader Jussi Halla-aho, we interviewed in 2015 and 2017); UK Conservatives (2): two MEPs; Polish Law and Justice (1): one MEP; Alternative for Germany (1): one MEP. ECR interviews were conducted in Brussels, Copenhagen and Strasbourg.

4. Camre told a Dutch TV station in 2009 that Muslims in Denmark behaved in a manner worse than the Nazis. He was convicted of racism in August 2015 for a 2014 tweet comparing Muslims to Hitler. See: https://www.thelocal.dk/20150818/danish-politician-racism-compared-muslims-to-hitler. For his comments on Romania and Bulgaria, see https://www.telegraph.co.uk/news/worldnews/europe/eu/5324440/Bulgarians-and-Romanians-not-intelligent-enough-to-make-decisions-for-the-EU.html

5. Bale et al. (2010: 97) commented in 2010 that if parties like the DF had been allowed to join the ECR, 'the liberal media in the United Kingdom would certainly find it very easy indeed to find ammunition to embarrass Mr Cameron—probably on a weekly, if not a daily, basis'.

6. Halla-aho says that it was the National Coalition Party in particular that lobbied for them to be declined by the ECR.

7. This situation changed for the Finns when they split in 2017 after Jussi Halla-aho's election as leader and only the less radical splinter group Blue Reform remained in the Finnish government.

8. Interestingly, Lorentzen notes that there is also an element of payback here for an incident that occurred in 2000 when the FPÖ were in national government and the DF were

still a pariah party. As he told us, one reason 'we didn't want the Freedom Party—the Austrian Freedom Party—to join the group was because they had been rejecting us back in 2000 when Pia Kjærsgaard, our chairman, and some people from the party, they travelled down to Vienna to visit, to show their support for Mr Haider, but they didn't want to meet people from the Danish People's Party'.

9. See the discussion in Jungar and Jupskäs (2014) about the wariness of the Finns Party leadership in those years, regarding connections with SD.
10. It is worth noting, however, that—despite these reservations expressed in our interviews—the DF in the previous EP had invited Wilders' party to apply for membership of the EFD group. While the PVV MEPs at the time were keen, Wilders vetoed the idea (see the next chapter).

## 4. EUROPE OF FREEDOM AND DIRECT DEMOCRACY: AN ACCEPTABLE MARRIAGE OF CONVENIENCE

1. Our interviews with the EFDD were as follows. UKIP (3): one MEP, one former senior official/press officer, and one senior advisor/official (whom we interviewed three times in 2014, 2015 and 2017); Five Star Movement (2): two MEPs who were leaders of the party's EP delegation; Sweden Democrats (2): one senior national party MP; 1 party official who was responsible for negotiating EP alliances. We also interviewed Peter Mach, the sole MEP from the Czech Party of Free Citizens. Interviews were conducted in Brussels, Strasbourg, Stockholm, and London.
2. See: http://www.europarl.europa.eu/pdf/grants/Grant_amounts_foundations%2003–2015_new%20logo.pdf

3. See: https://www.theguardian.com/politics/2018/may/30/defunct-eurosceptic-party-linked-to-ukip-asked-to-repay-11m
4. See the Reuters report here: https://www.reuters.com/article/us-dutch-wilders-moroccans/dutch-politician-referred-to-prosecutors-for-anti-moroccan-remarks-idUS-BREA2C1JS20140313
5. See https://sverigesradio.se/sida/artikel.aspx?programid=2054&artikel=5873904
6. For details of the M5S online vote for its EP group choice, see https://www.euractiv.com/section/uk-europe/news/five-star-movement-votes-online-to-join-farage-s-efd/
7. See https://www.metro.se/artikel/jimmie-%C3%A5kesson-v%C3%A4ldigt-tydligt-att-det-bl%C3%A5ser-v%C3%A4nstervindar-xr.

## 5. EUROPE OF NATIONS AND FREEDOM: A MARRIAGE OF LOVE?

1. Our interviews with the ENF parties were as follows. FN (5): two MEPs, two senior advisors/officials; one 2019 MEP candidate; VB (2): one MEP (whom we interviewed in 2014 and 2015) and the party leader; LN (3): one current MEP and two former MEPs; FPÖ (3): one former MEP, one MP and one senior European-level advisor. The PVV does not speak to academics, however we were able to conduct an extensive interview with the former PVV MEP (2009–14), Lucas Hartong, in 2015. ENF interviews were conducted in Brussels, Strasbourg, Vienna, Paris and Milan.
2. The speeches are available on the 'Lega Salvini Premier' Youtube account. Wilders: https://www.youtube.com/watch?v=arCuDYdEU_8&ab_channel=LegaNord

Padania; Annemans: https://www.youtube.com/watch?v=Fv0viILUWZU; De Danne: https://www.youtube.com/watch?v=tXUVfSW3I7Q; Strache: https://www.youtube.com/watch?v=OUp2uGvdne8

3. According to the European Parliament Directorate-General for Finance, the EAF in 2011 was awarded a maximum amount that year of €372,753. See: http://www.europarl.europa.eu/pdf/grants/grant_amounts_parties.pdf
4. https://euobserver.com/eu-elections/124158
5. Korwin-Mikke has expressed numerous highly controversial views including, during his 2014 EP campaign, the claim that 'there was no proof Hitler was aware of the Holocaust' and the assertion that 'the difference between rape and consensual sex was very subtle'. See: https://blogs.lse.ac.uk/europpblog/2014/06/10/the-congress-of-the-new-right-is-the-latest-anti-establishment-party-to-have-success-in-poland-but-it-may-struggle-to-secure-long-term-support/. This type of behavior continued after his election to the EP. See, for example, his use of the N-word in a parliamentary speech: http://www.thenews.pl/1/10/Artykul/176471,Polish-MEP-branded-racist-after-Europarliament-speech
6. See: https://www.lemonde.fr/politique/article/2015/06/13/le-fn-ecarte-jean-marie-le-pen-de-ses-statuts_4653491_823448.html
7. See the video of the full press conference here: https://www.youtube.com/watch?v=uq1zV6q1M-w
8. As the Vlaams Belang leader, Tom van Grieken, joked to us in 2015, they cannot very well say they are 'against Brussels' in the same way as the Front National and other parties can.

9. https://www.menleuropa.eu/.
10. E.g. https://www.fetedesnations.eu/.
11. https://www.opendemocracy.net/can-europe-make-it/cas-mudde/eaf-is-dead-long-live-menl, https://www.eumonitor.eu/9353000/1/j9vvik7m1c3gyxp/vjuzfubie8vp.
12. Whether Marine Le Pen has really succeeded in changing her party's more toxic elements is another question. See, for example, Mayer (2015) who argues that the new FN looks a lot like the old version in terms of its supporters' attitudes towards Muslims and Jews.
13. Hartong resigned from the PVV in 2014 because of the new alliance and the anti-Semitic reputation of some of the ENF parties. In our interview, he explained: 'Marine Le Pen is not a bad woman, I think. She is different from her father, but her father is a very anti-Semitic person. That for me was a red flag, and also the FPÖ from Austria was founded by some former Nazis and still there's a very strong undercurrent in ... within the party that is very focused against Israel, against Jewish people'.
14. Mölzer had been an important figure for many years in trying to bring European radical right parties together. See Mudde (2007: 180–181). Somewhat ironically given that their parties finally joined the same group, neither Mölzer nor Provera were MEPs in the 2014–19 Parliament. While Provera was not re-selected as a candidate (following Salvini becoming leader), Mölzer had to withdraw from the election in April 2014 following controversial and racist remarks made at a party meeting. See: https://www.ibtimes.co.uk/austrian-far-right-mep-andreas-molzer-quits-eu-elections-over-race-remark-1443922

15. Provera says that he was given responsibility for exploring foreign links by the LN leader, Umberto Bossi. According to him, 'We were nearly always in agreement, but it was a subject that was discussed very little within the party'.
16. We thank Marta Lorimer for directing us to this quote.

## 6. RADICAL RIGHT POPULISTS INSIDE AND OUTSIDE THE EUROPEAN PARLIAMENT

1. Collected 20 November 2018.
2. See, for example: https://www.theguardian.com/commentisfree/2013/jun/03/2014-european-elections-shape-eu
3. 29–08–2018—INTA_AD(2018)623884
4. 23–10–2017—A8–0321/2017
5. Belgium did not have a general election between July 2014 and April 2019, which rules out Vlaams Belang from this analysis. Press releases for the Danish People's Party in 2015 are not available.
6. See: https://www.fpoe.at/medien/pressemeldungen/
7. https://www.huffingtonpost.co.uk/2014/09/30/tories-eu-true-finns-conference_n_5905036.html?utm_hp_ref=uk&ir=UK
8. http://conservativeeurope.com/news/come-meet-us-at-party-conference/
9. A Spitzenkandidat is a group's candidate for European Commission President.
10. https://web.archive.org/web/20160122065246/http://addeurope.org/all-news
11. https://www.dw.com/en/europes-right-wing-parties-meet-near-vienna-urge-brexit/a-19339474

12. https://www.euractiv.com/section/future-eu/news/far-right-counter-summit-claims-europe-will-wake-up-in-2017; https://www.theguardian.com/world/2017/jan/21/marine-le-pen-leads-gathering-of-eu-far-right-leaders-in-koblenz
13. https://www.euractiv.com/section/elections/news/in-prague-europes-far-right-celebrates-the-austrian-coalition/
14. https://www.euractiv.com/section/future-eu/news/le-pen-seeks-to-rally-far-right-allies-for-european-elections/; https://www.independent.co.uk/news/world/europe/marine-le-pen-far-right-france-front-national-geert-wilders-pvv-salvini-lega-a8331396.html
15. E.g. https://www.cbsnews.com/news/european-far-right-germany-geert-wilders-marine-le-pen/; http://en.rfi.fr/europe/20140529-ukip-s-farage-front-national-s-le-pen-compete-eurosceptic-leadership-and-eu-cash; https://www.dagelijksestandaard.nl/2017/01/geert-wilders-frauke-petry-en-marine-le-pen-ontmoeten-elkaar-in-duitsland-gaan-voor-een-vrij-europa/.
16. E.g. https://pbs.twimg.com/media/B3tZK3uCMAEte7b.png.
17. https://brusselsdiplomatic.com/2016/01/29/marine-le-pen-met-salvini-in-milan-salvini-milan-immigration/
18. https://www.france24.com/en/20181008-le-pen-salvini-brussels-bunker-european-elections
19. https://www.geertwilders.nl/in-de-media-main-menu-74/nieuws-mainmenu-114/94-english/1957-wilders-le-pen-strache-and-salvini-in-the-wall-street-journal
20. See: https://ecrgroup.eu/article/ecr_group_approves_

two_new_members_peter_lundgren _and_kristina_winberg
21. See: https://www.theguardian.com/politics/2018/jul/04/tory-meps-criticised-alliance-with-swedish-populists-sweden-democrats
22. See: https://sverigesradio.se/sida/artikel.aspx?programid=2054&artikel=

## 7. FROM INTERNATIONAL POPULISM TO TRANSNATIONAL POPULISM

1. Farage spoke at a Trump campaign rally in Jackson, Mississippi, on 24 August 2016. See: https://www.youtube.com/watch?v=oj4K9fr_WgY He has also met and been photographed with Trump on other occasions; Salvini has expressed his support for Bolsonaro in various tweets and the latter has replied in kind. See, for example: https://twitter.com/matteosalvinimi/status/1049189100467773445?lang=en; https://twitter.com/matteosalvinimi/status/1056672554520375297?lang=en and https://twitter.com/jairbolsonaro/status/1073537603591376896?lang=en
2. The previous three waves were said to be 'Neo-Fascism, 1945–55' (e.g. parties like the Movimento Sociale Italiano—Italian Social Movement), 'Right-wing populism, 1955–80' (parties like that led by Pierre Poujade in France), and 'Radical Right, 1980–2000' (new parties like the Sweden Democrats and transformed parties like the Austrian Freedom Party). See Mudde (2019) and von Beyme (1988).
3. See: https://www.nytimes.com/2019/04/08/world/europe/italy-salvini-far-right-alliance.html
4. See: https://www.theguardian.com/politics/2019/may/

18/europe-far-right-leaders-unite-milan-vow-to-change-history
5. See: https://www.ft.com/content/010eec62-30b5-11e7-9555-23ef563ecf9a
6. See: http://espresso.repubblica.it/plus/articoli/2019/02/21/news/tre-milioni-matteo-salvini-russia-1.331924?preview=true
7. See: https://www.nytimes.com/2016/12/19/world/europe/austrias-far-right-signs-a-co-operation-pact-with-putins-party.html
8. https://www.sueddeutsche.de/politik/strache-video-fpoe-oesterreich-ibiza-1.4451784
9. Data from May 2019. See: https://www.dr.dk/nyheder/politik/vaelgervandringer#O2015
10. See: https://www.politico.eu/article/euroskeptic-dutch-party-aims-to-join-ecr-group-after-eu-election/
11. Kaczynski and Orbán held their first public meeting in Krynica (Poland) in September 2016. See: https://www.ft.com/content/e825f7f4-74a3-11e6-bf48-b372cdb1043a; Salvini and Orbán met in Milan in August 2018. See: https://www.politico.eu/article/viktor-orban-matteo-salvini-team-up-to-attack-emmanuel-macron/
12. In addition to the articles above, see the following about Orbán and Salvini's meeting: https://www.theguardian.com/world/2018/aug/28/matteo-salvini-viktor-orban-anti-migrant-plan-brussels
13. See: https://www.theatlantic.com/ideas/archive/2019/05/bernard-henri-levy-interviews-viktor-orban/589102/
14. See: https://www.youtrend.it/2018/12/13/sondaggi-politici-elettorali-tecne-13-dicembre-europa-italia-germania/
15. See: https://oegfe.at/2018/11/07_survey/

16. See: https://www.thelocal.dk/20190104/danish-eu-support-at-record-high-poll
17. https://www.bloomberg.com/news/articles/2018-06-29/two-out-of-three-swedes-want-to-remain-in-the-eu-poll-shows
18. See: https://www.aftonbladet.se/debatt/a/A2Kpyr/sd-darfor-andrar-vi-var-eu-politik
19. See: https://www.reuters.com/article/us-italy-politics-salvini/italys-salvini-changes-tack-on-eu-in-bid-for-center-ground-idUSKBN1OB224
20. See: https://www.thelocal.it/20190110/italys-salvini-calls-for-populist-european-spring
21. Although Mariani only formally announced his move to RN and his EP candidature in January 2019, we knew at the time of interview in November 2018 that this was likely to happen.
22. See: https://www.smh.com.au/opinion/selfpromotion-the-real-purpose-of-geert-wilders-antiislam-campaign-20151012-gk6l33.html

# BIBLIOGRAPHY

Akkerman, T., de Lange, SL. and Rooduijn, M. (2016) 'Inclusion and mainstreaming? Radical Right-Wing Populist Parties in the New Millennium', In: Akkerman, T., de Lange, SL. and Rooduijn, M. (eds.) *Radical Right-Wing Populist Parties in Western Europe: Into the Mainstream?*, New York: Routledge, pp. 1–28.

Albertazzi, D. and McDonnell, D. (2015) *Populists in Power*, London: Routledge.

Albertazzi, D., Giovannini, A. and Seddone, A. (2018) '"No Regionalism Please, We Are Leghisti!" The Transformation of the Italian Lega Nord Under the Leadership of Matteo Salvini', *Regional & Federal Studies*, 28 (5): 645–671.

Almeida, D. (2010) 'Europeanized Eurosceptics? Radical Right Parties and European Integration', *Perspectives on European Politics and Society*, 11 (3): 237–253.

Art, D. (2011) *Inside the Radical Right: The Development of Anti-immigrant Parties in Western Europe*, Cambridge: Cambridge University Press.

Arzheimer, K. (2018) 'Conceptual Confusion is not Always a Bad Thing: The Curious Case of European Radical Right Studies', In: Marker, K., Roseneck, M., Schmitt, A. and

Sirsch, J. (eds.) *Demokratie und Entscheidung*, Wiesbaden: Springer, pp. 23–40.

Bakker, R., et al. (2015) *1999–2014 Chapel Hill Expert Survey Trend File. Version 2015.1*. Available on chesdata. eu. Chapel Hill, NC: University of North Carolina, Chapel Hill.

Bale, T. (2006) 'Between a Soft and a Hard Place? The Conservative Party, Valence Politics and the Need for a New "Eurorealism"', *Parliamentary Affairs* 59 (3): 385–400.

Bale, T., Hanley, S. and Szczerbiak, A. (2010) '"May Contain Nuts"? The Reality Behind the Rhetoric Surrounding the British Conservatives' New Group in the European Parliament', *The Political Quarterly* 81 (1): 85–98.

Bolin, N. (2015) 'A Loyal Rookie? The Sweden Democrats' First Year in the European Parliament', *The Polish Quarterly of International Affairs* 11(2): 59–77.

Bornschier, S. (2011) 'National Political Conflict and Identity Formation: The Diverse Nature of the Threat from Extreme Left and Extreme Populist Right', In: Fuchs, D. and Klingemann, H.-D. (eds.) *Cultural Diversity, European Identity and the Legitimacy of the EU*, Cheltenham: Edward Elgar, pp. 171–200.

Brack, N. (2015) 'The Roles of Eurosceptic Members of the European Parliament and Their Implications for the EU', *International Political Science Review* 36 (3): 337–350.

――― (2017a) *Opposing Europe in the European Parliament: Rebels and Radicals in the Chamber*, London: Palgrave.

――― (2017b) 'Eurosceptic Members of the European Parliament. Foxes in the Henhouse?', In: Leruth, B., Startin, N. and Usherwood, S. (eds.) *The Routledge Handbook of Euroscepticism*, London: Routledge.

# BIBLIOGRAPHY

Bressanelli, E. (2012) 'National Parties and Group Membership in the European Parliament: Ideology or Pragmatism?', *Journal of European Public Policy* 19 (5): 737–54.

Bressanelli, E. and de Candia, M. (2018) 'Love, Convenience or Respectability? Understanding the Alliances of the Five Star Movement in the European Parliament', *Italian Political Science Review* 1–24.

Brunsbach, S., John, S. and Werner, A. (2012) 'The Supply Side of Second-Order Elections: Comparing German National and European Election Manifestos', *German Politics* 21 (1): 91–115.

Budge, I., Klingemann, H.-D., Volkens, A., Bara, J. and Tanenbaum, E. (2001) *Mapping Policy Preferences. Estimates for Parties, Electors, and Governments 1945–1998*. Oxford: Oxford University Press.

Canovan, M. (1981) *Populism*. New York: Harcourt Brace Jovanovic.

——— (2005) *The People*. Cambridge: Polity Press.

Chryssogelos, A. (2019) 'Salvini and Kaczynski—the New "Axis" Powers?' *EUobserver*, available at: https://euobserver.com/opinion/143948.

*Corriere della Sera* (2002) 'Troppa Gente di Sinistra, alla Farnesina è Ora di Cambiare', 24 April.

Decker, F. (2016) 'The "Alternative for Germany": Factors Behind its Emergence and Profile of a New Right-Wing Populist Party', *German Politics and Society* 34 (2): 1–16.

de Cleen, B. (2017) 'Populism and Nationalism', In: Rovira Kaltwasser, C., Taggart, P., Ochoa Espejo, P. and Ostiguy, P. (eds.) *The Oxford Handbook of Populism*, Oxford: Oxford University Press, pp. 342–362.

De Lange, S.L. (2007) 'A New Winning Formula? The

Programmatic Appeal of the Radical Right', *Party Politics* 13 (4): 411–435.

De Lange, S.L. and Art, D. (2011) 'Fortuyn Versus Wilders: An Agency-Based Approach to Radical Right Party Building', *West European Politics* 34 (6): 1229–1249.

Directorate-General for Finance (2018) *Funding from the European Parliament to Political Parties at European Level per Party and per Year*. http://www.europarl.europa.eu/pdf/grants/Funding_amounts_parties%2001–2018.pdf, accessed 3.12.2018.

Dittrich, P.-J. (2017) *Social Networks and Populism in the EU*, Jacques Delors Institut, Berlin.

ECR (2018) *Financial Statements European Conservatives and Reformists Group. Budget Item 400 of the Budget of the European Parliament. Financial Year Ending 31 December 2017*.

EFDD (2018) *Report by the EFDD Group in the European Parliament. Budget Item 400. 2017*.

Ellinas, A.A. (2015) 'Neo-Nazism in an Established Democracy: The Persistence of Golden Dawn in Greece', *South European Society and Politics* 20 (1): 1–20.

ENF (2018) *Report by the ENF Group in the European Parliament. Budget Item 400. 2017*.

Fieschi, C., Shields, J. and Woods, R. (1996) 'Extreme Right-Wing Parties and the European Union: France, Germany and Italy', In: Gaffney, J. (ed.) *Political Parties and the European Union*, London: Routledge, pp. 235–253.

Fieschi, C. (2000) 'European Institutions: The Far-Right and Illiberal Politics in a Liberal Context', *Parliamentary Affairs* 53 (3): 517–31.

Fitzgibbon, J. and Leruth, B. (2017) 'Conclusion' In:

Fitzgibbon, J., Leruth, B. and Startin, N. (eds.) *Euroscepticism as a Transnational and Pan-European Phenomenon*, London: Routledge, pp. 162–172.

Freeden, M. (1998) 'Is Nationalism a Distinct Ideology?' *Political Studies* 46 (4): 748–765.

Froio, C. and Ganesh, B. (2018) 'The Transnationalisation of Far-Right Discourse on Twitter', *European Societies*, published in 'early view online', 20 July 2018.

Garzia, D., Trechsel, A. and De Sio, L. (2017) 'Party Placement in Supranational Elections: An Introduction to the Euandi 2014 dataset', *Party Politics* 23 (4): 333–341.

Gemenis, K., (2013) 'What to Do (and Not to Do) with the Comparative Manifestos Project Data', *Political Studies* 61: 3–23.

Gidron, N. and Bonikowski, B. (2013) 'Varieties of Populism: Literature Review and Research Agenda', *Weatherhead Working Paper Series*, No. 13–0004. https://scholar.harvard.edu/gidron/publications/varieties-populism-literature-review-and-research-agenda

Heinisch, R. and Mazzoleni, O. eds. (2016) *Understanding Populist Party Organisation: The Radical Right in Western Europe*, London: Palgrave.

Hix, S., Noury, A. and Roland, G. (2005) 'Power to the Parties: Cohesion and Competition in the European Parliament, 1979–2001', *British Journal of Political Science* 35 (2): 209–234.

——— (2007) *Democratic Politics in the European Parliament*. Cambridge: Cambridge University Press.

Hooghe, L., Bakker, R., Brigevich, A., De Vries, C.E., Edwards, E.E., Marks, G.W. et al. (2010) 'Reliability and Validity of the 2002 and 2006 Chapel Hill Expert Surveys on Party Positioning', *European Journal of Political Research* 49 (5): 687–703.

Ivaldi, G. and Lanzone, M.E. (2016) 'The French Front National: Organizational Change and Adaptation from Jean-Marie to Marine Le Pen', In: Heinisch, R. and Mazzoleni, O. (eds) *Understanding Populist Party Organisation: The Radical Right in Western Europe*, London: Palgrave, pp. 131–158.

Ivarsflaten, E. (2006) '*Reputational shields: Why Most Anti-Immigrant Parties Failed in Western Europe, 1980–2005*', paper prepared for the 2006 Annual Meeting of the American Political Science Association in Philadelphia.

Jungar, A., and Jupskås, A.R. (2014) 'Populist Radical Right Parties in the Nordic Region: A New and Distinct Party Family?', *Scandinavian Political Studies* 37 (3): 215–238.

Kefford, G. and McDonnell, D. (2018) 'Inside the Personal Party: Leader-Owners, Light Organizations and Limited Lifespans', *British Journal of Politics and International Relations* 20 (2): 379–394.

Kitschelt, H. and McGann, A.J. (1995) *The Radical Right in Western Europe: A Comparative Analysis*. Ann Arbor: University of Michigan Press.

Kriesi, H. (2014) 'The Populist Challenge', *West European Politics* 37 (2): 361–378.

Le Pen, J-M (1984) *Les Français d'Abord*. Carrère Lafon.

Leruth, B. (2017) 'Is 'Eurorealism' the new 'Euroscepticism'? Modern Conservatism, the European Conservatives and Reformists and European integration', In: Fitzgibbon, J., Leruth, B. and Startin, N. (eds.) *Euroscepticism as a Transnational and Pan-European Phenomenon*, London: Routledge, pp. 46–62.

# BIBLIOGRAPHY

Leruth, B. (2018) 'Transnational and Pan-European Euroscepticism', In: Leruth, B., Startin, N. and Usherwood, S. (eds.) *The Routledge Handbook of Euroscepticism*, London: Routledge, pp. 384–396.

Lucardie, P. (2008) 'The Netherlands: Populism versus Pillarization', In: Albertazzi, D. and McDonnell, D. (eds.) *Twenty-First Century Populism*, London: Palgrave, pp. 135–150.

Marks, G.W., Hooghe, L., Nelson, M. and Edwards, E.E. (2006) 'Party Competition and European Integration in the East and West: Different Structure, Same Causality', *Comparative Political Studies* 39 (2): 155–75.

Marks, G.W., Hooghe, L., Steenbergen, M.R., and Bakker, R. (2007) 'Crossvalidating Data on Party Positioning on European Integration', *Electoral Studies* 26 (1): 23–38.

Maurer, A., Parkes, R. and Wagner, M. (2008) 'Explaining Group Membership in the European Parliament: The British Conservatives and the Movement for European Reform', *Journal of European Public Policy* 15 (2): 246–62.

Mayer, N (2015) 'Le Mythe de la Dédiabolisation du FN'. *La Vie des Idées*, 1–9. Available at: https://hal.archives-ouvertes.fr/hal-01312408/document

McDonnell, D. (2006) 'A weekend in Padania: Regionalist Populism and the Lega Nord', *Politics* 26 (2): 126–132.

McDonnell, D. and Vampa, D. (2016) 'The Italian Lega Nord', In: Heinisch, R. and Mazzoleni, O. (eds.) *Understanding Populist Party Organisation: The Radical Right in Western Europe*, London: Palgrave, pp. 105–129.

McDonnell, D. and Werner, A. (2018a) 'Respectable Radicals: Why Some Radical Right Parties in the European Parliament Forsake Policy Congruence', *Journal of European Public Policy* 25 (5): 747–763.

# BIBLIOGRAPHY

McDonnell, D. and Werner, A. (2018b) 'Differently Eurosceptic: Radical Right Populist Parties and Their Supporters', *Journal of European Public Policy*, published in 'early view online', 23 December.

McElroy, G. and Benoit, K. (2010) 'Party Policy and Group Affiliation in the European Parliament', *British Journal of Political Science* 40 (2): 377–98.

——— (2011) 'Policy Positioning in the European Parliament', *European Union Politics* 1 (1): 150–67.

Mény, Y. and Y. Surel. 2002. 'The Constitutive Ambiguity of Populism.' In: Mény, Y. and Surel, Y. (eds.) *Democracies and the Populist Challenge*, London: Palgrave, pp. 1–21.

Minkenberg, M. and Perrineau, P. (2007) 'The Radical Right in the European Elections 2004', *International Political Science Review* 28 (1): 29–55.

Minkenberg M. (2017) *The Radical Right in Eastern Europe: Democracy under Siege?* New York: Palgrave Macmillan.

Moffitt, B. (2017) 'Transnational Populism? Representative Claims, Media and the Difficulty of Constructing a Transnational "People"', *Javnost—The Public* 24 (4): 409–425.

Mudde, C. (2007) *Populist Radical Right Parties in Europe*. New York: Cambridge University Press.

———(2016) *The Study of Populist Radical Right Parties: Towards a Fourth Wave*, C-Rex Working Paper Series, no. 1.

———(2017). 'Populism: An Ideational Approach', In: Rovira Kaltwasser, C., Taggart, P., Ochoa Espejo, P. and Ostiguy, P. (eds.) *The Oxford Handbook of Populism*, Oxford: Oxford University Press, pp. 179–194.

———(2019) *The Far Right Today*. Cambridge: Polity Press.

Müller, W.C. and Strøm, K. (1990) 'Political Parties and Hard Choices', In: Müller, W.C. and Strøm, K. (eds.) *Policy, Office or Vote. How Political Parties in Western Europe Make Decisions*, Cambridge: Cambridge University Press, pp. 1–35.

Müller, J-W. (2016) *What is Populism?* Philadelphia: University of Pennsylvania Press.

Netjes, C.E., and Binnema, H.A. (2007) 'The Salience of the European Integration Issue: Three Data Sources Compared', *Electoral Studies* 26 (1): 39–49.

Otjes, S., Ivaldi, G., Jupskås, A.R. and Mazzoleni, O. (2018) 'It's not Economic Interventionism, Stupid! Reassessing the Political Economy of Radical Right-wing Populist Parties', *Swiss Political Science Review* 24 (3): 270–290.

Pirro, A.L.P. (2015) *The Populist Radical Right in Central and Eastern Europe: Ideology, Impact, and Electoral Performance*. London: Routledge.

Pirro, A.L.P., Taggart, P. and van Kessel, S. (2018) 'The Populist Politics of Euroscepticism in Times of Crisis: Comparative Conclusions', *Politics* 38 (3): 378–390.

Polk, J., et al. (2017) 'Explaining the Salience of Anti-Elitism and Reducing Political Corruption for Political Parties in Europe with the 2014 Chapel Hill Expert Survey Data', *Research & Politics* 4 (1): 1–9.

Pytlas, B. (2016) *Radical Right Parties in Central and Eastern Europe: Mainstream Party Competition and Electoral Fortune*. London: Routledge.

Reif, K. and Schmitt, H. (1980) 'Nine Second-Order elections—A Conceptual Framework for the Analysis of European Election Results', *European Journal of Political Research* 8 (1): 3–44.

# BIBLIOGRAPHY

Rooduijn, M., Van Kessel, S., Froio, C., Pirro, A., de Lange, S.L., Halikiopoulou, D., Lewis, P., Mudde, C. and Taggart, P. (2019) *The PopuList: An Overview of Populist, Far Right, Far Left and Eurosceptic Parties in Europe*. Available at: https://popu-list.org/

Röth, L., Afonso, A. and Spies, D. (2018). 'The Impact of Populist Radical Right Parties on Socio-Economic Policies', *European Political Science Review* 10 (3): 325–350.

Rydgren, J. (2008) 'Sweden: The Scandinavian Exception', In: Albertazzi, D. and McDonnell, D. (eds.) *Twenty-First Century Populism*, London: Palgrave, pp. 135–150.

Schmitt, H., Braun, D., Popa, S., Mikhaylov, S. and Dwinger, F. (2018) *European Parliament Election Study 1979–2014, Euromanifesto Study*. GESIS Data Archive, Cologne. ZA5102 Data file Version 2.0.0, doi:10.4232/1.12830.

Settembri, P. (2004) 'When is a Group Not a Political Group? The Dissolution of the TDI Group in the European parliament', *The Journal of Legislative Studies* 10 (1): 150–74.

Shekhovtsov, A. (2017) *Russia and the Western Far Right: Tango Noir*, London: Routledge.

Stanley, B. (2008) 'The Thin Ideology of Populism.' *Journal of Political Ideologies* 13 (1): 95–110.

Stanley, B., and Cześnik, M. (2019) 'Populism in Poland', In: Stockemer, D. (ed.) *Populism Around the World*, Cham: Springer, pp. 67–87.

Startin, N. (2010) 'Where to for the Radical Right in the European Parliament? The Rise and Fall of Transnational Political Co-Operation', *Perspectives on European Politics and Society* 11 (4): 429–49.

Startin, N. and Brack, N. (2017) 'To Co-Operate or Not to

Co-Operate? The European Radical Right and pan-European Co-Operation', In: Fitzgibbon, J., Leruth, B. and Startin, N. (eds.) *Euroscepticism as a Transnational and Pan-European Phenomenon*, London: Routledge, pp. 42–59.

Taggart, P. (2004) 'Populism and Representative Politics in Contemporary Europe', *Journal of Political Ideologies* 9 (3): 269–288.

Taggart, P. and Szczerbiak, A. eds. (2008) *Opposing Europe? The Comparative Party Politics of Euroscepticism, Volume 1: Case Studies and Country Surveys*. Oxford: Oxford University Press.

Tarchi, M. (2013) 'What's Left of the Italian Right?', *Studia Politica* 13 (4): 693–709.

*The Guardian* (2008) '"I Don't Hate Muslims. I Hate Islam" Says Holland's Rising Political Star', 16 February.

Usherwood, S. and Startin, N. (2013) 'Euroscepticism as a Persistent Phenomenon', *Journal of Common Market Studies* 51 (1): 1–16.

Usherwood, S. (2016) 'The UK Independence Party: The Dimensions of Mainstreaming', In: Akkerman, T., de Lange, S.L. and Rooduijn, M. (eds.) *Radical Right-Wing Populist Parties in Western Europe: Into the Mainstream?* London: Routledge, pp. 247–267.

Van Kessel, S., and Castelein, R. (2016) 'Shifting the Blame: Populist Politicians' Use of Twitter as a Tool of Opposition', *Journal of Contemporary European Research* 12 (2): 594–614

Vasilopoulou, S. and D. Halikiopoulou (2015) *The Golden Dawn's 'Nationalist Solution': Explaining the Rise of the Far Right in Greece*. London: Palgrave.

Vasilopoulou, S. (2018) 'The Radical Right and Euroskepticism', In: Rydgren, J. (ed.) *The Oxford Handbook of the Radical Right*, Oxford: Oxford University Press, pp. 122–140.

Volkens, A. (2007) 'Strengths and Weaknesses of Approaches to Measuring Policy Positions of Parties', *Electoral Studies* 26 (1): 108–120.

Volkens, A., Werner, K., Lehmann, P., Matthieß, T., Merz, N., Regel, S. and Weßels, B. (2018) *The Manifesto Data Collection. Manifesto Project (MRG/CMP/MARPOR). Version 2018b*. Berlin: Wissenschaftszentrum Berlin für Sozialforschung (WZB).

von Beyme, K. (1988) 'Right-Wing Extremism in Post-War Europe', *West European Politics* 11 (2): 1–18.

Vossen, K. (2017) *The Power of Populism: Geert Wilders and the Party for Freedom in the Netherlands*. London: Routledge.

Werner, A., Lacewell, OP. and Volkens, A. (2014) *Manifesto Coding Instructions: 5th fully revised edition*. Berlin: Wissenschaftszentrum Berlin für Sozialforschung (WZB).

Whitaker, R. and Lynch, P. (2014) 'Understanding the Formation and Actions of Eurosceptic Groups in the European Parliament: Pragmatism, Principles and Publicity', *Government and Opposition* 49 (2): 232–63.

# INDEX

Åkesson, Jimmie, 120, 132, 221
Aliot, Louis, 212
Alleanza Nazionale, 43, 194, 198
Alliance for Direct Democracy in Europe (ADDE), 106–7, 133, 182, 185
Alliance of Conservatives and Reformists in Europe (ACRE), 70, 106, 182–3
Alliance of Liberals and Democrats for Europe (ALDE), 57, 59, 86
Alternative for Germany, *see* Alternative für Deutschland
Alternative für Deutschland (AfD), 5, 6, 58, 60, 72, 124, 180, 186, 187, 206, 207
Annemans, Gerolf, 132, 135, 136, 146, 152, 154, 155, 186
anti-Semitism, 84, 123, 146, 159
Atkinson, Janice, 136
Austria
   coalition government (2017–19), 25, 27, 220
   Euroscepticism, 220
   immigration, 228
   legislative election (1999), 44
   legislative election (2017), 25, 52, 152, 180, 209
   Südtirol, 32
Austrian Freedom Party, *see* Freiheitliche Partei Österreichs

'Basta Euro' tour (2014), 221–2
Belders, Bas, 77, 95

# INDEX

Belgium
   Nieuw-Vlaamse Alliantie (N-VA), 58
   Vlaams Belang (VB), *see* Vlaams Belang
   Vlaams Blok (VB), 29
Berlusconi, Silvio, 25, 34
Blue Reform, 214
Bolsonaro, Jair, 197
Bonino List, 30
Bontes, Louis, 147
Borrelli, David, 113, 119
Bossi, Umberto, 33–4, 132–3
Brexit, 11, 17, 185, 186, 189, 208, 215, 220, 230

Cameron, David, 55
Camre, Mogens, 74
Chapel Hill Expert Survey, 8, 13, 44, 45–6, 61, 97, 129, 137, 158, 201–2
   on economic views, 66, 90, 104–5, 112, 140–41
   on European integration, 61, 63, 80, 90, 99–101, 112, 137–9
   on immigration, 65, 90, 101–3, 112, 139–40
   on social views, 66, 90, 103–4, 112, 140–41

Chauprade, Aymeric, 135, 146, 156
Christian Democratic Union of Germany, 28
Christian Democrats, 3
Chrysí Avgí, 5, 22
Churchill, Winston, 199
coalition theory, 34, 36
'coalitionability', 43–4
communism, 21
Conference of Presidents, 41, 107
Conservative Party (UK), 4, 8, 10, 11, 15, 49, 50, 53, 55–61, 64–8, 89–91, 198
   Brexit, 11, 17, 189, 208, 215
   Dansk Folkeparti, 72–9, 81–2, 85, 90–91, 163, 178, 182, 184, 199, 205, 208
   economic views, 66, 68
   European integration, 61, 76, 89
   immigration, 64, 65, 75–6
   leadership election (2005), 55
   Perussuomalaiset, 72, 73–5, 76–8, 81, 90–91, 178, 182, 208

# INDEX

rapporteur positions, 173
social views, 66
Sverigedemokraterna, 10, 11, 78, 79, 85, 179, 188–9, 190
UKIP, 27–8, 78
voting cohesion, 168
Conservative People's Party of Estonia, 207
*cordons sanitaires*, 28, 43, 152
Corrao, Ignazio, 114, 167
Council of the European Union, 37, 222
Counter Summit (2017), 153, 180, 186
Czarnecki, Ryszard, 75, 84, 213

D'Hondt method, 41
Danish People's Party, *see* Dansk Folkeparti
Dansk Folkeparti (DF), 1, 4, 7, 10, 11, 14–15, 25, 31, 51, 199, 214–15
Conservative Party, 72–9, 81–2, 85, 90–91, 163, 178, 182, 184, 199
economic views, 67–9, 90

EAPN, 206, 207, 215
ECR, *see* Dansk Folkeparti in ECR
EFDD, 15, 53, 57–61, 68, 69, 71, 72, 76, 79–82
ENF, 82–8, 90, 91
European elections (2014), 52, 201
European integration, 62–4, 80, 220
Euroscepticism, 24, 79, 90
Freiheitliche Partei Österreichs, 83, 91, 110, 123, 209, 210
Front National, 15, 59, 83–4, 91, 134, 146
Identity and Democracy, 207–8, 215
immigration, 64, 74, 75–6, 79, 90
international populism, 157
Partij voor de Vrijheid, 59, 86, 110–11
Perussuomalaiset, 179
Prawo i Sprawiedliwość, 209
racism, 85
rapporteur positions, 173–6

## INDEX

reputational shield, 214
respectable marriage,
  81–2, 88–9, 94–5,
  161, 163, 178, 183–4,
  198, 204, 208, 211
Russia, 213
social views, 67–9, 90
Sverigedemokraterna,
  10, 11, 83, 85–6, 117,
  121–2, 179, 189–94,
  205, 208
taxation, 79
UKIP, 80, 91, 107, 154,
  184–5
Vlaams Belang, 83, 86,
  123
Dansk Folkeparti in ECR,
  10, 11, 14, 15, 50, 53,
  57–91
  Conservative Party,
    72–9, 82, 85, 90–91,
    163, 178, 182, 184,
    199, 208
  respectable marriage,
    81–2, 88–9, 94–5,
    161, 163, 178, 183–4,
    198, 204, 208, 211
  voting cohesion, 168
De Danne, Ludovic,
  131–2, 133, 135, 146,
  211, 212

Denmark
  Dansk Folkeparti (DF),
    see Dansk Folkeparti
  Euroscepticism, 220–21
Dewinter, Filip, 132

Eesti Konservatiivne Rah-
  vaerakond (EKRE), 207,
  222
Ekeroth, Kent, 50, 120,
  121, 122, 133
Ethniki Politiki Enosis
  (EPEN), 29
Eurobarometer, 223–8
Europarties, 16, 70, 106,
  107, 120, 133, 143–4,
  182
Europe of Democracies and
  Diversities, 93
Europe of Freedom and De-
  mocracy (EFD), 93
  Dansk Folkeparti, 15, 53,
    57–61, 68, 69, 71, 72,
    76, 79–82, 90, 110
  Freiheitliche Partei Ös-
    terreichs, 110
  Laikós Orthó doxos
    Synagermós, 94
  Lega Nord, 110, 128
  Partij voor de Vrijheid,
    110–11, 128

264

# INDEX

Perussuomalaiset, 15, 53, 57–61, 68, 69, 71, 72, 79–82, 90, 110
UKIP, 39, 57, 61, 68, 69, 72, 75, 78, 80, 81, 94–5, 96, 110, 128, 185
voting cohesion, 167
Europe of Freedom and Direct Democracy (EFDD), 4–5, 7, 13, 14, 15, 16, 30, 49, 93–126
ADDE, 106–7, 133, 182, 185
Brexit, 185
Dansk Folkeparti, 15, 53, 57–61, 68, 69, 71, 72, 76, 79–82, 90
European election (2014), 52
European integration, 99–101
financial resources, 70, 105
group-related events, 180, 185
immigration, 101–3
marriages of convenience, 94, 108–26, 153, 162
office spoils, 105–8, 203–4

Partij voor de Vrijheid, 111–12
policy congruence, 44, 98–105
rapporteur positions, 173, 176
stability, 187–8, 195
as staging post, 98, 121, 124, 154, 164
voting cohesion, 165, 166–7, 168, 170–72
Europe of Nations and Freedom (ENF), 4–5, 10, 13, 15, 16, 30, 49, 61, 69, 127–60
Counter Summit (2017), 153, 180, 186
Dansk Folkeparti, 82–8, 90, 91
European election (2014), 52
European identity, 155–7, 159–60
European integration, 99–101, 109, 138
financial resources, 105
group-related events, 180, 185–7, 199
Hague press conference (2013), 2, 131–2
immigration, 102, 109, 139–40

265

## INDEX

Islam, 131, 156
Kongres Nowej Prawicy, 134, 135–6
marginalisation, 150–51, 159, 199
MENF, 143–4, 182
office spoils, 142–4, 158
Perussuomalaiset, 82–8, 90, 91
policy congruence, 44, 128, 129–30, 136–42, 158, 162, 203, 211
proud populists, 149–55, 164, 197
rapporteur positions, 173, 177
Russia, 213
stability, 187–8, 195
Sverigedemokraterna, 10, 99, 101–5, 120–25, 132–4, 154, 191
transnational populism, 157–8, 219
voting cohesion, 166, 168–72
European Alliance for Freedom (EAF), 120, 133
European Alliance of Peoples and Nations (EAPN), 206–7, 215
European Commission, 37
European Conservatives and Reformists (ECR), 4–5, 6, 7, 13, 16, 30, 49, 55–91, 216
ACRE, 70, 106, 182–3
Brexit, 189
European election (2014), 52
European integration, 55, 56, 57, 61–4, 67, 80
financial resources, 70
group-related events, 180, 182–3
immigration, 64–6
office spoils, 69–71, 204
policy congruence, 44, 53, 59, 60–69, 79, 90
rapporteur positions, 173
respectable marriage, 81–2, 88–9, 94–5, 161, 163, 178, 183–4, 198, 204
stability, 187–94, 195
voting cohesion, 165, 166, 168, 170–71
European Council, 37, 222
European identity, 155–7, 159–60

# INDEX

European integration, 14, 23, 24, 50
  ECR, 55, 56, 57, 61–4, 67, 68, 80, 85, 89–90
  EFDD, 99–111, 115
  ENF, 99–101, 109, 138, 139, 144, 168, 191, 203
  *see also* Euroscepticism
European National Union (ENU—'Euronat'), 32–3
European People's Party (EPP), 6, 28, 43, 55, 57, 165, 194, 198, 217, 228
European refugee crisis (2015), 160, 223–8
European Socialists (PES), 29
European United Left (GUE), 29, 31, 166
Euroscepticism, 8, 22, 23–4, 39, 45, 52, 56–7, 76, 220–21
  Brexit, 220
  Conservative Party, 61, 76, 89
  Dansk Folkeparti, 68, 79, 220
  ECR, 68, 85, 89–90
  EFDD, 99–111, 115
  ENF, 139, 168, 191
  Front National, 24, 99, 138, 203, 221, 222–3
  international populism, 170, 194, 201
  Lega Nord, 99, 220
  Movimento Cinque Stelle, 99, 220
  transnational populism, 203, 210, 214, 220
  UKIP, 24, 80, 99, 100, 101, 104, 108, 109, 112–13
Eurozone, 24, 113, 148, 220, 221

Farage, Nigel, 95
  DF, 184–5
  FN, 155
  LN, 149
  PVV, 111–12
  PS, 74–5
  SD, 116
  Trump, 197
  visibility, 98, 114–15
Fidesz, 5, 6, 216–18, 222
Finland
  Blue Reform, 214
  parliamentary election (2015), 44, 52
  Perussuomalaiset (PS), *see* Perussuomalaiset

# INDEX

Finns Party, *see* Perussuomalaiset
First Czech Russia Bank, 212
Five-Star Movement, *see* Movimento Cinque Stelle
Flemish Interest, *see* Vlaams Belang
Fontana, Lorenzo, 152, 155
Forum voor Democratie (FvD), 216
Fox, Ashley, 188–9
Fox, Liam, 55
France
    European election (2014), 52
    Frexit, 188
    Front National (FN), *see* Front National
    Macron presidency (2017–), 217
    presidential election (2017), 25, 52, 187–8, 221, 222
    Rassemblement National, 228
Francois, Mark, 55
Freedom and Direct Democracy, 207
Freiheitliche Partei Österreichs (FPÖ), 5, 7, 25, 27, 33, 43–4, 50
    coalition government (2017–19), 25, 27, 220
    'coalitionability', 43–4
Dansk Folkeparti, 83, 91, 110, 123, 209, 210
EAF, 120, 133
economic views, 141
ENF, *see* Freiheitliche Partei Österreichs in ENF
European election (2014), 52
Euroscepticism, 24, 99, 100, 101, 138, 203
Front National, 128, 144, 178, 180
Identity, Tradition and Sovereignty, 30, 33
Identity and Democracy, 207–8
Islam, 156, 203
Lega Congress (2013), 132, 134
Lega Nord, 110, 149
legislative election (1999), 44
legislative election (2017), 25, 152, 180, 209

# INDEX

marginalisation, 150
non-inscrit, 31, 142
Partij voor de Vrijheid, 34, 111, 128
Perussuomalaiset, 83, 91, 110, 123, 210
Prawo i Sprawiedliwość, 84
proud populists, 149–55, 164, 197
Russia, 212–13
Sverigedemokraterna, 10, 123–4, 154
transnational populism, 157–8
UKIP, 110, 123
Freiheitliche Partei Österreichs in ENF, 110, 128, 129, 158
    Lega Congress (2013), 132, 134
    marginalization, 150
    office spoils, 142
    policy congruence, 203
    voting coherence, 168
Front National (FN), 1, 2, 5, 7, 25, 27, 33, 51, 53
    anti-Semitism, 123, 146–8, 159, 205
    *cordon sanitaire* against, 28, 43
    Dansk Folkeparti, 15, 59, 83–4, 91, 134, 146
    *dédiabolisation*, 130, 146, 159, 178, 205
    EAF, 120, 133
    ENF, *see* Front National in ENF
    European elections (2014), 200–201
    European National Union, 32–3
    Euroscepticism, 24, 99, 138, 203, 221, 222–3
    Fidesz, 217
    Freiheitliche Partei Österreichs, 128, 144, 178, 180
    group-related events, 186–7, 194, 199
    Hague press conference (2013), 2, 131–2
    Identity, Tradition and Sovereignty, 30, 33
    immigration, 64, 186, 203
    Jobbik, 6, 134, 135
    Kongres Nowej Prawicy, 134, 135–6
    leadership, 25, 130, 136, 145–8, 159, 204–5
    Lega Congress (2013), 132, 134

Lega Nord, 33–4, 53, 94, 128, 144, 159, 178
non-inscrit, 31, 142
Partij voor de Vrijheid, 34, 53, 94, 111, 127–8, 144, 146–7, 159
Perussuomalaiset, 15, 59, 83–4, 91, 134
presidential election (2017), 25, 187–8, 221, 222
proud populists, 149–55, 164, 197
rapporteur positions, 177
Russia, 212, 213
Sverigedemokraterna, 10, 120, 122–3, 205
UKIP, 14, 53, 97, 108, 109–10, 134, 155
Vlaams Belang, 146
Vlaams Blok, 29
Front National in ENF, 2, 53, 61, 64, 97, 109, 127–40, 158
*dédiabolisation*, 130, 146, 159
group-related events, 186–7, 194, 199
Hague press conference (2013), 131–2
Jobbik, 134, 135
Kongres Nowej Prawicy, 134, 135
leadership change, 130, 136, 145–8, 204–5
Lega Congress (2013), 132, 134
office spoils, 142
policy congruence, 137–42, 203
UKIP, 155
voting coherence, 168
funding, 3, 27, 39, 40, 45, 70, 106–7, 142–4, 204

Gauche unitaire européenne (GUE), 29, 31, 166
Germany, 58
Alternative für Deutschland (AfD), 5, 6, 58, 60, 72, 124, 180, 186, 187, 206, 207
Christlich Demokratische Union (CDU), 28
Republikaner, Die, 29
Sozialdemokratische Partei Deutschlands (SPD), 29
global financial crisis (2007–8), 23

# INDEX

Golden Dawn, *see* Chrysí Avgí
Gollnisch, Bruno, 32, 136, 149
Greece, 58
   Chrysí Avgí (Golden Dawn), 5, 22
   Ethniki Politiki Enosis (EPEN), 29
   Laikós Orthó doxos Synagermós (LAOS), 94
   Syriza, 29
Greens, 3, 166
group formation, 34

Haider, Jörg, 34
Halla-Aho, Jussi, 79, 81, 83, 86, 87, 173, 190–93, 199, 210, 213
Hannan, Daniel, 50, 73–4, 76, 77, 78, 85, 192
Hartong, Lucas, 51, 110–11, 147
Helmer, Roger, 110, 112
Henkel, Hans-Olaf, 72
Hübner, Johannes, 146, 211
Huhtasaari, Laura, 207

Identity and Democracy (ID), 207–8, 215, 216
Identity, Tradition and Sovereignty (ITS), 30, 32, 39
immigration, 21, 23, 43, 45, 160, 223–8
   EAPN, 207
   ECR, 64–6, 74, 75–6, 79
   EFDD, 101–3
   ENF, 102, 109, 139–40, 203
   Eurobarometer, 223–8
   refugee crisis (2015), 160, 223–8
   transnational populism, 210, 211, 214, 217, 219, 223
Initiative for Direct Democracy, 106
international populism, 16, 17, 131, 157, 206, 218–19, 223
Islam, 16, 21, 131, 207, 228, 229
   DF, 74, 86–7
   FPÖ, 156
   PVV, 23, 86–7, 111–12, 133, 203, 229
   UKIP, 111–12
Italy
   Alleanza Nazionale (AN), 43, 194, 198

# INDEX

Alto Adige, 32
Bonino List, 30
Euroscepticism, 220, 221
general election (2013), 222
general election (2018), 25, 52, 152, 180, 209
immigration, 228
Lega Nord, *see* Lega Nord
Movimento Cinque Stelle (M5S), *see* Movimento Cinque Stelle
Movimento Sociale Italiano (MSI), 29, 43
Partito Democratico (PD), 29

Jobbik Magyarországért Mozgalom, 5, 6, 134, 135, 216
Jomshof, Richard, 50, 122, 123, 189–90

Kaczynski, Jaroslaw, 216–18, 220
Karlsson, Mattias, 215–16
Klaus, Václav, 132
Koblenz Counter Summit (2017), 153, 180, 186

Kongres Nowej Prawicy (KNP), 134, 135–6
Korwin-Mikke, Janusz, 134, 135
Kotro, Olli, 206

Laikós Orthó doxos Synagermós (LAOS), 94
Law and Justice, *see* Prawo i Sprawiedliwość
Le Pen, Jean-Marie, 32, 34, 61, 84, 110, 123, 130, 146–8, 157
Le Pen, Marine, 1, 2, 84, 95, 109–10, 123, 133–4, 135, 145–8
 *dédiabolisation*, 130, 146, 159, 204–5
 ENF, formation of (2013–15), 2, 61, 94, 109, 131
 Facebook, 229
 Farage, relationship, 155
 father, relationship, 147–8
 group-related events, 186–7, 194, 199
 international figure, 229
 national differences, 32
 Orbán, 217
 presidential election (2017), 222

# INDEX

Salvini, 152
Sverigedemokraterna, 120, 134
leadership, 1, 25, 26, 130, 145–9
Lebreton, Gilles, 177
Lega Nord (LN), 1, 5, 7, 24, 25, 27, 31, 32, 33–4, 221–2
'Basta Euro' tour (2014), 221–2
Council of the European Union, 222
'cultural counter-revolution', 216–18, 220
EAPN, 206, 207
EFD, 110, 128
ENF, *see* Lega Nord in ENF
European election (2014), 52
European integration, 99, 138, 203, 220, 221
Fidesz, 216–18
Freiheitliche Partei Österreichs, 110, 149
Front National, 33–4, 53, 94, 128, 144, 159, 178
general election (2013), 222
general election (2018), 25, 152, 180, 209
group-related events, 186–7, 194, 199
immigration, 203, 217
leadership, 25, 145, 148–9, 159, 204
marginalisation, 150, 152
Partij voor de Vrijheid, 94
proud populists, 149–55, 164, 198
rapporteur positions, 177
refugee crisis (2015), 223
Russia, relations with, 212
UKIP, 149
Lega Nord in ENF, 109, 128–32, 136, 152, 160
leadership, 148–9
marginalisation, 150, 152
policy congruence, 203
Turin Congress (2013), 132, 134
voting cohesion, 168
Lijst Pim Fortuyn (LPF), 25

273

# INDEX

Lorentzen, Karsten, 80, 85, 87
Lundgren, Peter, 119, 177

Mach, Petr, 115, 167
Macron, Emmanuel, 217
mainstreaming, 200
manifestos, 46–7
marginalisation, 150–51, 159
Mariani, Thierry, 228
Maroni, Roberto, 132, 148
marriages of convenience, 3, 11, 94, 108–26, 153, 162
Marusik, Michał, 136
Messerschmidt, Morten, 50
   ECR, 71, 72, 74, 76, 77, 82, 173–6, 184
   EFD, 71, 76, 111
   FN, 84
   PiS, 209
   PVV, 86
   racism conviction (2002), 74
   rapporteur positions, 173–6
   SD, 122, 179
Meuthen, Jörg, 206
Modi, Narendra, 230
Mölzer, Andreas, 133, 150

Montel, Sophie, 188
Movement for a Europe of Nations and Freedom (MENF), 143–4, 182
Movimento Cinque Stelle (M5S), 4, 8, 11, 49, 95, 96, 98–107, 108, 109, 126
   economic views, 103–5, 112
   European integration, 99, 100, 220
   immigration, 101, 102, 103, 112
   rapporteur positions, 176
   social views, 103–5, 112
   Sverigedemokraterna, 119
   UKIP, 112–15
   voting cohesion, 167
Movimento Sociale Italiano (MSI), 29, 43
Mussolini, Alessandra, 32

nationalism, 4, 15, 22, 31–3, 128
National Front (France), *see* Front National
Nazism, 84, 85, 121
neo-Nazism, 84, 85, 121

# INDEX

Netherlands
  Forum voor Democratie (FvD), 216
  general election (2017), 52
  Islam, 23, 87, 111–12, 133, 203, 229
  Lijst Pim Fortuyn (LPF), 25
  Partij voor de Vrijheid, *see* Partij voor de Vrijheid
  Socialistische Partij, 29
Nieuw-Vlaamse Alliantie (N-VA), 58
non-inscrits, 3, 6, 30, 31, 40, 48, 142
Nordic Council, 216
Nordic Green Left (NGL), 29, 31, 166
Northern League, *see* Lega Nord

Občanská Demokratická Strana (ODS), 56–61, 64–7, 68, 89, 168, 183
office spoils, 38–41, 45, 48
  ECR, 69–71, 204
  EFDD, 105–8, 203–4
  ENF, 142–4, 158
Okamura, Tomio, 186

Olivier, Philippe, 222–3, 230
Orbán, Viktor, 216–18, 220

Paksas, Rolandas, 78
Partij voor de Vrijheid (PVV), 2, 5, 7, 12, 25, 31
  *cordon sanitaire*, 28
  Counter Summit (2017), 180, 186
  Dansk Folkeparti, 59, 86, 110–11
  economic views, 104, 141
  EAPN, 207
  EFD, 110–11
  EFDD, 111–12
  ENF, *see* Partij voor de Vrijheid in ENF
  European election (2014), 52
  Euroscepticism, 24, 80, 99, 138, 203
  Freiheitliche Partei Österreichs, 34, 111, 128
  Front National, 34, 53, 94, 111, 127–8, 144, 146–7, 159
  group-related events, 186–7, 194, 199
  Islam, 23, 86–7, 111–12, 133, 203, 229

# INDEX

leadership, 25, 145, 159, 204
Lega Nord, 94
marginalisation, 151
and MENF, 144
non-inscrit, 142
Perussuomalaiset, 59, 87
proud populists, 12, 149–55, 164, 197
Vlaams Belang, 146
Partij voor de Vrijheid in ENF, 2, 61, 109, 127–9, 138, 141, 158, 160
   Counter Summit (2017), 180, 186
   Front National, 146–7, 159
   Hague press conference (2013), 2, 131–2
   Lega Congress (2013), 132, 134
   MENF, 144
   policy congruence, 203
   voting cohesion, 168
Partija Tvarka ir Teisingumas (PTT), 93, 96
Party for Freedom (Netherlands), *see* Partij voor de Vrijheid
Perussuomalaiset (PS), 4, 7, 10, 11, 14, 31, 199
   'coalitionability', 44
   Conservative Party, 72, 74–8, 81, 90–91, 163, 178, 182, 199
   Dansk Folkeparti, 179
   economic views, 67–9, 90
   EAPN, 206, 207, 215
   ECR, *see* Perussuomalaiset in ECR
   EFDD, 15, 53, 57–61, 68, 69, 71, 72, 79–82, 90
   ENF, 82–8, 90, 91
   European integration, 62–4, 80, 90
   Freiheitliche Partei Österreichs, 83, 91, 110, 123, 210
   Front National, 15, 59, 83–4, 91, 134
   Identity and Democracy, 207–8, 215
   immigration, 64, 90
   international populism, 157
   leadership, 214
   Partij voor de Vrijheid, 59, 87
   rapporteur positions, 173

# INDEX

reputational shield, 81
respectable marriage,
    81–2, 88–9, 94–5,
    161, 163, 178, 183,
    198, 204, 208
Russia, 213
social views, 67–9, 90
Sverigedemokraterna,
    10, 11, 83, 86, 179,
    190–94
UKIP, 74–5, 80–81, 91
Vlaams Belang, 83, 86,
    123
Perussuomalaiset in ECR,
    14, 15, 50, 53, 57–91,
    94–5, 161, 163, 168
    Conservative Party, 72,
        74–8, 81, 90–91, 163,
        178, 182, 199, 208
    respectable marriage,
        81–2, 88–9, 94–5,
        161, 163, 178, 183,
        198, 204, 208
    voting cohesion, 168
Philippot, Florian, 188
Pim Fortuyn List, 25
Podemos, 29
Poland
    Kongres Nowej Prawicy
        (KNP), 134, 135
    Prawo i Sprawiedliwość
        (PiS), *see* Prawo i
        Sprawiedliwość
policy congruence, 37–9,
    44, 45–8, 201–3
    ECR, 44, 53, 59, 60–69,
        79, 90
    EFDD, 44, 98–105
    ENF, 44, 128, 129–30,
        136–42, 158, 162,
        203, 211
Prague Declaration (2009),
    56
Prawo i Sprawiedliwość
    (PiS), 5, 6, 56–61, 72,
    75, 89, 209
    Council of the European
        Union, 222
    'cultural counter-revolution', 216–18
    Dansk Folkeparti, 209
    EAPN, 207
    economic views, 66, 67,
        68
    European integration,
        63, 64
    Fidesz, 216–18
    Identity and Democracy,
        215
    immigration, 64, 65
    rapporteur positions, 173
    Russia, 84, 213

# INDEX

social views, 66, 67, 68
voting cohesion, 168
Pretzell, Marcus, 187
proud populists, 12,
    149–55, 164, 197, 200
Provera, Fiorello, 150
Putin, Vladimir, 17, 84,
    212, 215, 230

rapporteurs, 39, 41, 48,
    108, 143, 163, 172–7
Rassemblement National,
    228, *see* Front National
refugee crisis (2015), 160,
    223–8
reputational shields, 43, 81,
    88, 121, 214, 217
'respectable marriage'
    theory, 11, 60, 88–9, 91,
    98, 120, 161, 163, 204
    Dansk Folkeparti, 81–2,
        88–9, 94–5, 161, 163,
        178, 183–4, 198, 208
    Perussuomalaiset, 81–2,
        88–9, 94–5, 161, 163,
        178, 183, 198, 208
    Sverigedemokraterna,
        85, 98, 120–21, 164,
        189, 198
respectable radicals, 14, 15,
    198, 200, 208, 211, 216,
    217, 229

Romania, 32, 74
Russia, 17, 78, 84, 212–13,
    217, 230

Salvini, Matteo, 1, 94,
    130–31, 132–3, 145,
    148–9, 153, 204
    'Basta Euro' tour (2014),
        221–2
    EU reform, 216–18,
        220, 221
    Fidesz, 216–18
    group-related events,
        186–7, 194, 199
    Russia, 212
Sarkozy, Nicolas, 228
Schweizerische Volkspartei
    (SVP), 27
Sinn Féin, 29
Sked, Alan, 125
Soini, Timo, 74–5, 182,
    184, 193
Speroni, Francesco, 148–9
*Spitzenkandidat*, 183
Strache, Heinz-Christian,
    132, 186–7, 212
Strana Svobodných
    Občanů (SSO), 115, 167
Strøm, Kaare, 13, 35–7,
    203
Südtirol, 32

# INDEX

Sverigedemokraterna (SD), 4, 7, 10–12, 14, 31, 69, 79
  Conservative Party, 10, 11, 78, 79, 85, 179, 188–9, 190, 205
  *cordon sanitaire*, 28, 43
  Dansk Folkeparti, 10, 11, 83, 85–6, 117, 121–2, 179, 189–94, 205, 208
  EAF, 120, 133
  EAPN, 207
  ECR, *see* Sverigedemokraterna in ECR
  EFDD, *see* Sverigedemokraterna in EFDD
  ENF, 10, 99, 101–5, 120–25, 132–4, 154, 191
  European integration, 99, 100, 101, 104, 191
  Freiheitliche Partei Österreichs, 10, 123–4, 154
  Front National, 10, 120, 122–3, 205
  general election (1998), 120, 189
  general election (2018), 222

Identity and Democracy, 215–16
immigration, 64, 102, 103, 117
international populism, 157
mainstreaming, 200
marginalisation, 151
Movimento Cinque Stelle, 119
Perussuomalaiset, 10, 11, 83, 86, 179, 190–94
racism, 79, 117–19, 192, 205
respectable marriage, 85, 98, 120–21, 164, 189, 198, 204, 211
Russia, 213, 215
social views, 103–4
UKIP, 11, 14, 53, 78, 97, 115–19, 124–5, 154, 178, 189
Sverigedemokraterna in ECR, 7, 10, 11, 16, 50, 78, 134, 164, 179, 188–95
  respectable marriage, 85, 98, 120–21, 164, 189, 198, 204, 211
Sverigedemokraterna in EFDD, 7, 11, 16, 53, 64, 78, 95, 96, 115–25, 134

office spoils, 105–7
policy congruence, 98–105
respectable marriage, 98, 120–21, 211
UKIP, 11, 14, 53, 78, 97, 115–19, 124–5, 154, 178
voting cohesion, 167
Svoboda a Prímá Demokracie (SPD), 207
Sweden
general election (2014), 11, 44, 52
general election (2018), 11, 189, 222
Sweden Democrats, *see* Sverigedemokraterna
Syriza, 29

Technical Group of Independents, 29, 35, 39
Terho, Sampo, 80, 87, 214
Thatcher, Margaret, 199
Thulesen Dahl, Kristian, 1, 76
*Towards a Common Sense Europe! Peoples Rise Up* (2019), 206
Towler, Gawain, 111–12, 114, 124

transnational populism, 16, 17, 131, 157–8, 160, 206, 218–30
Trump, Donald, 197, 230

UK Independence Party (UKIP), 4, 7, 11, 14, 27, 31, 50, 64, 69, 78, 93–119, 165, 167
ADDE, 107, 185
Brexit, 17, 185
'coalitionability', 44
Conservative Party, 27–8, 78, 90
Dansk Folkeparti, 80, 91, 107, 154, 184–5
economic views, 104, 112, 202
ECR, 90
EFD, 39, 57, 61, 68, 69, 72, 75, 78, 80, 81, 94–5, 96, 110, 128
ENF, 14, 96, 99, 101, 102, 104, 105, 106, 109–12, 136, 154–5
European election (2014), 52, 201
Euroscepticism, 24, 80, 99, 100, 101, 104, 108, 109, 112–13
Freiheitliche Partei Österreichs, 110, 123

INDEX

Front National, 14, 53, 97, 108, 109–10, 134, 155
general election (2015), 107, 109, 112
immigration, 64, 101–2, 103, 109, 112
international populism, 157
Lega Nord, 149
MPs, 27–8
office spoils, 106, 107, 143
parliamentary work, 76, 80, 107, 165, 176
Perussuomalaiset, 74–5, 80–81, 91
public orators, 98, 108, 114
social views, 103–4, 112
Sverigedemokraterna, 11, 14, 53, 78, 97, 115–19, 124–5, 154, 178, 189
Vlaams Belang, 123
United Kingdom
Brexit, 11, 17, 185, 186, 189, 208, 215, 220, 230
European election (2014), 52
general election (2015), 44, 75, 78, 107, 109, 112
United Russia, 212–13

Van Grieken, Tom 153–4
Van Orden, Geoffrey, 50, 55, 56, 73, 75, 76, 78
Vilimsky, Harald, 186
Vistisen, Anders, 83, 208
ECR, 182, 183
EFD, 81–2, 183
FPÖ, 84–5, 209, 210
SD, 85, 190–92
Vlaams Belang (VB), 5, 7, 32, 51
*cordon sanitaire*, 28, 43, 152
Dansk Folkeparti, 83, 86, 123
European election (2014), 52
European integration, 99, 100, 101, 138, 203
Identity, Tradition and Sovereignty, 30, 33
Identity and Democracy, 207–8
immigration, 64, 203
Lega Congress (2013), 132, 134

marginalisation, 152, 199
non-inscrit, 31, 142
Partij voor de Vrijheid, 146
Perussuomalaiset, 83, 86, 123
proud populists, 149–55, 164, 197
Vlaams Belang in ENF, 64, 128, 129, 132, 134, 158
  Front National, 146
  marginalisation, 152, 199
  policy congruence, 203
  voting cohesion, 168
Vlaams Blok (VB), 29
Volya, 207
Von Storch, Beatrix, 187
vote-seeking, 42–4, 45, 204
VoteWatch, 51, 163, 166, 167
voting cohesion, 164–72
Vox, 216

*Wall Street Journal*, 187
welfare state, 21, 45, 67, 104
Wilders, Geert, 2, 25, 86, 131–3, 145, 146–7, 152, 159, 204
  Counter Summit (2017), 180, 186
  EFD, invitation to join (2011), 111
  EFDD, enquiry on joining (2014), 111–12
  ENF, formation of (2013–14), 2, 61, 94, 109, 131
  group-related events, 186–7, 194, 199
  Islam, 23, 86–7, 111–12, 133, 229
  Israel, 146
  Le Pen Snr, 146–7
Winberg, Kristina, 119

Zahradil, Jan, 183
Żółtek, Stanisław, 136